Praise for
The Healing Power of African American Spirituality

"Traditional African Spirituality in itself is inherently rebellious—a delicious roux, an okra gumbo for the beautiful black soul. Stephanie Rose Bird's emotionally liberating text champions the syncretism of diasporic healing motifs while enhancing the potency of eclectic African-centered folklore. As you travel the pages of this book you will begin to conjure change in your own life by any herb/bath root or oil at your disposal. You will triumphantly follow the cowrie shells back to the crossroads lined with deities happy to be both nappy and, above all, sun kissed."

—**Mawiyah Kai EL-Jamah Bomani,**
author of the plays *Spring Chickens* and *Crows Feet*

"*The Healing Power of African American Spirituality* by the illustrious Stephanie Rose Bird is a timely and much-needed inclusive contribution to humanity's spiritual awakening and evolution. Ms. Bird gives us richly textured, detailed descriptions and powerful histories about numerous, authentic African, African American, and Caribbean spiritual traditions and holistic health cures for the mind, body, and soul. Each Afro-centric culture Bird discusses offers their own uniquely captivating and sparkling messages about how to live one's best, magickal life inspired by the ancient beauty and truth of African spirituality. If you want to deepen and diversify your spiritual practice, you must add this book and Bird's other titles to your collection."

—**Ifeanyi C. Oshun,**
author of *Cats, Cauldrons, and Corsets* and owner of *Imaginateıııı.com*

THE HEALING POWER OF AFRICAN AMERICAN SPIRITUALITY

A Celebration of Ancestor Worship, Herbs and Hoodoo, Ritual and Conjure

The HEALING POWER OF AFRICAN AMERICAN SPIRITUALITY

STEPHANIE ROSE BIRD

author of *Sticks, Stones, Roots & Bones*

HAMPTON ROADS

Cover design by Kathryn Sky-Peck

Cover art *Paradise,*
2011 © Tamara Natalie Madden / Bridgeman Images

Interior by Steve Amarillo / Urban Design, LLC
Typeset in Addington CF, Berthold Akzidenz Grotesk BE, and Afolkalips

Hampton Roads Publishing Company, Inc.
Charlottesville, VA 22906
Distributed by Red Wheel/Weiser, LLC
www.redwheelweiser.com

Sign up for our newsletter and special offers by going
to *www.redwheelweiser.com/newsletter.*

ISBN: 978-1-64297-028-9
Library of Congress Cataloging-in-Publication Data
available upon request.

Printed in the United States of America
IBI
10 9 8 7 6 5 4 3 2 1

DEDICATION

For my ancestors

ACKNOWLEDGMENTS

Every book is the result of a collaborative effort. In the case of this book, a great deal of creative energy and positive thinking as well as hands-on help was shared by a wide variety of people. I wish to thank Greg Brandenburgh for shepherding this project from its inception. I am grateful to the incredible team of proofreaders, editors, designers, and PR and marketing experts at Hampton Roads Publishing for their help, which has been so essential to the making and publication of this book. Special thanks to my eagle-eyed personal editor and assistant, Jannette Giles, for her attention to detail and thoughtful input. I thank my first reader—my husband Damian—and my children, Colin, Liam, Olivia, and Ian, for their patience, love, and support while I was working on this project. I am grateful also to Ron and Iris Bird, my in-laws, for believing in my talents even when I did not and for being supportive as I wrote these pages. Thanks to my parents and community of elders, including my grandparents, uncles, and aunts, for instilling belief in creativity, an appreciation for nature, and the roll-up-your-sleeves, can-do spirit that is a hallmark of black people.

Ashe!

CONTENTS

THE HEALING POWER OF AFRICAN AMERICAN SPIRITUALITY

INTRODUCTION

From a young age, I was interested in all things considered dark and macabre, metaphysical, and what we've come to know as the mind body spirit connection. My work focuses on a particular aspect of healing that wants a place at the table and has much to contribute to the conversation. This work revolves around the intersection of my African ancestry and the African American culture I was raised in, and the age-old though contemporary, magickal and spiritual healing ways that stem from this deep well. My passion for this topic stems from curiosity about African-centered spiritual beliefs. I am called to them, from my center.

I have published seven books, including the COVR award-winning, *Sticks, Stones, Roots and Bones*. My books explore anthropology, healing, folklore, mythology, and magickal spirituality. *The Healing Power of African American Spirituality* brings all of these subjects together and takes a deep dive into them. By its very nature and intent, this is an eclectic book, which makes sense because I am an eclectic pagan. You will not find devotion to a singular path in these pages; the unifying element is the wisdom and guidance of the ancestors—a spiritually alive and evolving force.

I seek to situate African American healing in its rightful place in the lexicon of American and other healing traditions. In films and in some novels, black spiritual practices do seem to fall into that category of interest I first mentioned—the macabre—when in reality, that is not their holistic nature. Once you delve deeply into the varied continental African healing and spiritual practices, those influenced by sub-Saharan African healers, the people from which many of us descendants of slaves hold ancestry, a new picture develops.

African American spiritual practices, outside Abrahamic religions, have been little understood, but over the years they have become more clearly defined and distinctive. Once, our spiritual practices from the Motherland were outlawed, punishable by state-condoned torture and death. These ways have persisted through the Middle Passage and enslavement period, to freedom; they are alive and within us into the present day. Miraculously, they have not only survived, but continue to grow and evolve. In the pages of this book I delight in the rich array of Africanisms, spiritual practices that are found in our food-ways, song-ways, art-ways, and dance-ways. These unique practices are flourishing today.

As an herbalist and aromatherapist, my practice, and thus my writing, focuses on plants. Here, I explore African diasporic practices and beliefs that have a footing in the world of spirit through an engagement with plant magick and lore. This predilection for the spirituality of plants imbues this book with an eclectic African-centered vision that encompasses disparate belief systems that are connected through a genesis in the wide and diverse areas of both sub-Saharan and continental Africa.

This book is an exploration into African and African American spirituality, with a locus firmly situated in spiritual healing. When a bright light is flashed on the inequities and brutality my people suffer, such as the murders of George Floyd and Breonna Taylor at the hands of those entrusted to protect and save us from trouble, the need for African-inspired spirituality is especially strong.

Hoodoo, a largely African American group of folkloric practices, deals with everyday and common concerns. Specific herbs, which are called roots in the practice, come together with water and other natural elements to yield results. Hoodoo offers the ability to act on issues such as justice and social justice, which are challenging to address on the physical plain. It is an important part of this book because it breeds hope now, when we need it most.

My goal is to not only cultivate understanding and appreciation for black spirituality and healing ways but also to take its understanding and practice a step further. By presenting history, along with contemporary practices, my hope is to inspire and equip you to draw from this deep well of wisdom, working from where you stand.

Our practices are vibrant. They evolve as they continue to grow. This is my contribution to a folkloric and spiritual group of practices, centered around natural objects and most of all—plants, with strong roots in the Motherland.

How to Use this Book

How does one utilize a book that covers so much territory? To tap the wisdom of the ancestors, the Sankofa (pronounced *SAHN*-koh-fah) bird is a fitting symbol. From the Twi language of some people of Ghana, it represents the idea that you must look back at all you've been and all you've learned, and then look ahead to a more spirituality blessed future. This is the power in the image of Sankofa and it can be your power too. Sankofa is associated with the proverb, "It is not wrong to go back for what you have forgotten." This book provides you with some such opportunity.

I know it's difficult to do all of this, in our challenging times, but it doesn't hurt to try.

Read this book with curiosity and an open heart.

Take breathers to reflect on everything you've taken in.

Meditate on potential applications of what you've read, to add to your daily life.

Practice the types of work most meaningful to you, be they domestic, healing, for love, for abundance and prosperity, or cleansing.

Adapt and continue to grow.

Note: While this book covers some historical and traditional practices, I do not advocate for killing animals in ritual or using animal parts in our work for both legal and ethical reasons. As a vegetarian and environmentalist I believe it's important to protect animals and our fragile environment.

CHAPTER 1

AFRICAN AMERICAN SPIRITUALITY: AN OVERVIEW

frican American spirituality is a complex subject because its origins stretch across borders and touch on many different cultures. In this chapter, we examine African American spirituality as it is influenced by various African and Caribbean practices. We explore basic concepts in the lexicon of African earth-based spirituality such as *ashe, àṣẹ, nyama,* and *daliluw,* and in so doing find expanded meaning for the term we typically use to refer to nature being alive with spirit—animism.

Africanisms

Africanisms are African derived or inspired cultural practices present in traditions, language, and beliefs of a related culture, such as the African descended people of the Americas and Caribbean.

This first chapter is a journey into the heart of earth-based spirituality as it presents itself in Africa and the diaspora. It is designed to help readers who not only simply want to understand these practices but also those who want to become practitioners of African-styled earth-based spirituality, master the concepts behind these practices, understand Africanisms, and appreciate the deep connection our spirituality has to continental Africa and various locales in the African diaspora. To get to the heart of this eclectic group of practices, we must consider the term often applied to African American practices—soul. We start by looking at the African relationship to spirit.

Spiritual Terms: ATRs and ADRs

African traditional religions (ATRs) are the original (pre-Christian, pre-Islamic) religions of the indigenous sub-Saharan African people and include the Ile Ifa of the Yoruba people.

African derived religions (ADRs) are the types of spiritual practices found in the African diaspora and include Santeria, Obeah, Lucumi, Regla de Ocha, Orisa, and Quimbois.

A Boundary-less Spirituality

Many African Americans are descendants of sub-Saharan cultures that honor spirit as alive within nature. This includes the well-defined corpus of beliefs held by the Yoruba on the path of Ile Ifa, the cosmology of the Igbo, the shamanism of the Zulu and neighboring groups of Southern Africans, the wise griots, jelis, and priests of Bamana further northwest, and the healers of Democratic Republic of Congo from which many African Americans descend. All of these and other diverse groups' colorful belief systems were shared on the slave ships for generations, spilling over onto New World soils, filling our thoughts with the capability of seeing the universe and, indeed, certain objects as alive, powerful, and filled with potentiality.

Crossing cultural boundaries is a normal part of life for many multicultural people from our earliest history in the Americas. We speak various tongues, whether an officially recognized language or Creole, patois, tribal language, or perhaps a colloquial language of our homes and neighborhoods that differs from what is taught in schools. As we travel through life communicating with various people in ways that seem most appropriate, we resist the fixed linguistic and spiritual spaces or boxes that are often imposed on us.

Where in the World?

Afro-Caribbean
British Caribbean
French Caribbean

The Banishing and Survival of Sacred Rites

When my people were enslaved and brought to the United States, they quickly learned that speaking of nature spirit (spirits of nature such as trees, mountains, bodies of water, and stones) was a "no-no" punishable even by death. Eventually, African traditional religions (ATRs) and African derived religions (ADRs) were made illegal in the United States and parts of the Caribbean; such incursions have even been made recently in various parts of Africa.

Rather than communicate their beliefs to each other or with other cultures, enslaved Africans adapted their language to the Christian or Islamic faith of the dominant culture. In their healing work in the Americas and the Caribbean, they incorporated prayers of the dominant faith while maintaining various elements of African traditional spirituality (ATRs and ADRs). The scripture from the Holy Bible often masked the ATRs in the Christian cloak of the Protestants or Catholics, that is, an "acceptable" religion. Rather than describing herbs as being imbued with spirit or a healer as being connected to the spirit of nature, practitioners described the connections as coming from the Christian God. In this way, healing remained sacred work, but it was communicated in a language more acceptable to the mainstream instead of the language associated with ATRs.

When newly freed people of color began pressing for political and economic representation in both the British and French Caribbean islands, they were subdued first and foremost through their religious practices. For example, Obeah and Quimbois were suppressed or made illegal in the French Caribbean. During this time, one could be persecuted simply for practicing either religion, which those with power considered both dangerous and superstitious. These organized efforts to interfere with Obeah and Quimbois prevented practitioners from openly observing their ancestral rituals, ceremonies, and priestly duties.

There has always been a strong sense of survival underlining African Caribbean spirituality, however. Though these traditions were temporarily underground, they have survived to the present day.[1] Despite the best efforts to destroy connections to African traditional religion, there remains in the African diaspora a cultural perspective that healing using natural objects such as minerals and stones; various parts of plants; and animal teeth, bones, and skins is sacred because *everything* in nature is imbued with spiritual power.

Spiritual Terms

Babalawo—a healer/priest of Ile Ifa, "keeper of secrets"

Orisha—a deity in the Yoruba Ile Ifa cosmology

Oshun—Orisha of beauty, sensuality, and freshwater

Padrino—godfather/spiritual parent in Santeria or Ifa

Shango—fire, trickster Orisha in Yoruban pantheon

Yemaya-Olokun—Mother/Father of the sea in the
Yoruba pantheon; Yemaya is the upper ocean goddess
and Olokun the deep-sea god.

Quimbois, Obeah, Shango, Vodou, Myal, Hoodoo, Lucumi, and Regla de Ocha (the religion of the Orisha) continue in the African diaspora because they fill a vital function in black society: the ability to address the physical and spiritual realm as well as the environment in a way that reflects traditional African healing.

The Broad Spectrum of African American Spirituality

In thinking of spirit in a Western context, healing, prayer, invocation, and the church naturally come to mind. Like most Africans and African descended people, my family has close ties to organized religion, and, in fact, my maternal grandmother was a spiritualist minister of a Holiness Church. My second father, however, was a babalawo of Shango. My uncle, a drummer and a well-respected priest who did healing energy work, was a spiritual padrino of sorts to me and became one of the most influential figures in my spiritual life.

The following are a few of the ways and concepts through which African spirituality has survived into today.

Ancestor Spirits

In Haiti's Vodou, the Ghede are a family of spirits. In parts of West Africa and on the path of Ifa, *Egun* (which translates as "bones") refers to spirits. Both Ghede and Egun refer to the spirits of the ancestors, those who have passed on. Many of us among the living realize that these spirits are a guiding force in everyday life as well as sacred activities, thus we erect and maintain altars in remembrance of them. We visit with the ancestors in our dreams and vision quests, inviting their energy to bless medicinal blends so that they are infused with their spirit of goodwill, which will provide potent healing energy that grows from their connection with a wide array of entities. This is a very important facet of African-inspired healing work and holistic health.

Magickal Herbalism

When undertaking magickal herbalism for holistic health, honoring the pot, fire, candle, and tree as living entities with souls is essential. This is used cross-culturally throughout Africa and the African diaspora. Magick with a *k* is the art and science of causing change according to one's intention, which is distinct from the magic of illusion.

Neopaganism

Understanding our past is critical to our ability to self-heal our communities today. In neopaganism and fused paths, it is still important to preserve and disseminate the older ways of thinking because they offer a distinctive vision of the universe that remains viable. Engagement with ATRs and ADRs helps us maintain a spiritual connection with our planet as well as contact with our ancestors, who mediate between humans, gods, goddesses, nature spirits, and the creator being herself on our behalf.

Shamanism

Shamanism encompasses an array of traditional beliefs and practices found around the world with a major emphasis on communication with the spirit world. Shamanism has existed for thousands of years and is still practiced today. A practitioner of shamanism is known as a shaman. Shamans address matters of the mind, body, and spirit in the community, home environment, and individual. They are intermediaries between the human and spirit worlds. They can treat illness and are capable of entering supernatural realms to provide assistance to their clients. In sub-Saharan Africa, the shaman, who is often a hunter or warrior, heals by knowing and applying the collective power and proper mixture of plants and the elements. Here the term "shaman" is less common; the person who performs these practices is more often called a warrior, hunter, midwife, or healer. Around the world, shamans go by a variety of names and vocations.

Spiritual Concepts and Practices

The following are concepts and practices important to understanding the manifestation of spirit and soul in African cultures.

Animism and Ashe

Animism is the belief that natural objects are alive and have a spirit and soul.

Through an animistic lens, there is an important purpose for us once we make that final journey over into the realm of the spirit. In death, we continue to be honored by our family and ancestors and continue to have a vital role in our communities. As spirits, we live free of the constraints that society or even a corporeal body previously imposed on us.

In our ceremonial and ritual life, we experience natural and supposedly inanimate objects as alive because of this guiding belief in animism. This belief also allows us to meld more easily into the environment, coexisting meaningfully with the seasons, traveling freely with the Wheel of the Year, becoming as one with nature. We travel into the spirit realm through ecstatic dance, chant, and special songs, or with the aid of potent herbal medicines prepared by specialists.

In some regions of the world, however, particularly in West Africa, you are much more likely to see the word *ashe* used in conjunction with African shamanism rather than the word *animism*. *Ashe* means the invisible power of nature. It is a West African word that describes magical forces and energies of the universe. Ashe is present in nature, herbal preparations, and art made from natural materials. Herbal teas, incense powders, spiritual washes, healing balms, soap, charms, medicine bundles, and even the purposefully spoken word contain ashe. The Igala people of Nigeria, for example, consider any type of plant life to be filled with both medicinal power and the knowledge required to cure disease. Medicines, whether designed to address spiritual or physical complaints, are believed to derive their power from ashe.

Power Objects

What we consider African Art often serves a utilitarian purpose within sub-Saharan African communities. For example, power objects, which are shields, masks, sculptures, amulets, or charms, are all gifted by the power and energy of natural spirit. Each power object is a conglomeration of different elements of ashe. For example, both the Bamani Komo Society masks and Boli figurative sculptures are encrusted with feathers and quills. The mystical powers of the bird and porcupine are bound through wrapping and tying with string, thus encouraging them to share their unique ashe with the object. Encrustation is the result of people feeding the power object and demonstrates its life force; the object becomes encrusted with its power food. To remain alive and powerful, the objects must be fed.

THE WELL-FED OBJECT

Food is an important tool, for it sustains the life and empowers the soul of the magickal object. Traditionally, a power object may have been fed by applying ground stones or plants; leaves; feathers; ground bones; the skins, teeth, sexual organs, or horns of powerful animals; chicken blood; saliva; or even semen.

Medicine Bags

A medicine bag is a collection of power objects contained in a pouch or bag. It is charged through feeding an infinite variety of natural materials, though some are manmade, including glass and gunpowder. The best examples of these magical figures or accumulative sculptures come from Central Africa. The Yaka, Suku, and Kongo peoples prepare sachets made from shells, baskets, pots, bottles, food tins, plastic bags, or leather bags.

The Bamana of the Western Sudan use power objects such as medicine bags that are imbued with ashe for addressing various ills. These objects are used to express warrior power, to fight super-natural malaise, and to foil evil intentions. The bags contain *bilongo* (medicine) and a *mooyo* (a soul).

Other materials encased in a mojo bag include ephemera associated with the dead: coffin nails, ground bones, or graveyard dirt. The objects—whether stick, stone, leaf, or bone—have a corresponding spirit (ancestral, deity, or natural) and particular medicinal language ascribed to it.

Soul Bags

One can well imagine enslaved Congo and Angolan medicine people bringing the concept of bilongo and mooyo together in the New World to produce what we call mojo bags or soul bags. In addition to the conceptual connection of mooyo as soul, there is the visual connection between the words *mooyo* and *mojo,* which may suggest that the latter is an Anglicized translation.

In Hoodoo practice, mojo bags are prepared by a specialist akin to the *nganga* (healer or priest/priestess; plural, *banganga*), called in English a rootworker or conjurer. With the aid of their soul food, the individual objects within each bag become a cumulative force that guides the spirits to understand the reason their help is sought.

Nkisi/Minkisi

Nkisi is a Kongo power figure (*minkisi* is the plural). Ne Kongo, a cultural hero, carried the first healing medicines (minkisi) with him from heaven to earth. He prepared the medicines in a clay pot, set on top of three stones or termite mounds, creating the widely held belief that a healer (nganga) needed to create and dispense medicine.

Minkisi include elemental objects, representative of land, sky, fire, and water. Minkisi, also called charms, are empowered by the spirit of nature. These figures help people heal and can serve as a safe spot or hiding place for the soul. They might contain seashells, feathers, nuts, berries, stones, bones, leaves, roots, or twigs. Minkisi are as diverse and plentiful as the types of illnesses that exist on Earth.

A *nkisi nkondi*, for example, is a figure into which nails are inserted to bind the figure's powers. Leaves and medicine, combined with various elements, increase the strength. Each ingredient has an action on humans, and the bringing together of various natural forces becomes a source of healing.

In another form of empowering feeding, the Yaka, Kongo, Teke, Suku, and Songhai pack a cavity in the belly of their sculptures with a wide array of ashe-containing materials: bones, fur, claws, and elephant footprints; crocodile teeth, scales, and sexual organs' lightning excreta; bones, flesh, and nails of sorcerers; and remnants of suicide victims and of warriors. The figurines are covered with the skins of power animals (buffalo, wild cats, lizards, antelope, and birds) and then decorated with raffia, cloth, bells, beads, metal, and nails.

Daliluw

All of this mixing of disparate elements requires skill and knowledge that border on the metaphysical. Daliluw are the series of recipes and techniques for mixing the various medicinal constituents. Herbal chemistry is used, but some daliluw require spoken healing words, also called *àṣẹ*, and other metaphysical rituals during preparation. A West African word that translates roughly as "spiritual blessing," *àṣẹ* refers to when an illness is addressed directly in its own language. Another meaning is the use of powerful herbs that are chewed ritualistically as the power words (aṣe) are spoken. The ritualistic element enhances the daliluw by activating or controlling the energies that animate the world—animism.

Healer's Terms

Àṣẹ–spiritual blessing
Ashe–the invisible power of nature
Bilongo–medicine
Mooyo–soul
Nganga–healer, priest/priestess; plural, banganga

Jiridon and Tree Whispering

As a spiritual practice, Jiridon recognizes that trees are not only alive and contain spirit but are also teachers and can pass their knowledge on to sensitive humans. Rather than learn through an apprenticeship with a human healer, the seeker can learn directly from the trees and plants. To learn the art of Jiridon, the seeker, whether hunter, warrior, healer, or shaman, must spend ample amounts of time alone in the wilderness observing the workings of nature, including the expression of animals and the whispering of trees. Jiridon could be called "the science of the trees."

In early African American historical accounts, there are written testaments of people who spoke the language of the trees. They were called tree whisperers. Tree whisperers in the United States spend time living with and studying a single tree.

Qualities of Tree Whisperers

> Tree whisperers are highly observant.
> They are willing to forgo community life for a time.
> They listen attentively to the reactions the tree has to the lashing of wind and to warm sunny days.

Outcome of Study with Trees

> Eventually, the tree whisperer hears the studied tree speak clearly.
> The tree teaches those who will listen to be Masters of Jiridon.
> Masters of Jiridon become Master Empirical Herbalists and adept ecologists through metaphysical research.

Bringing Spirit Home

Organic objects are replete with potentiality and healing ashe, so they have a universal energy force within, connecting us all like an umbilical cord connects a fetus to its mother. It is important to address each element or aspect of nature with the assertion that it is alive and our partner. This approach puts us in touch at once with the past, present, ancestors, and nature spirits. Knowing we share stewardship with a living world, which we do not own but are a component of, allows us to move more easily toward a spiritually rich, sustainable future. Borrowing practices from the complex realm of African spirituality helps build new traditions and spiritual practices that put us in touch with the spirit realm enriching our soul.

Healer's Terms

Master Empirical Herbalist–one who masters understanding of the herbal kingdom through observation and self- or spiritually directed experiments rather than through scientific assay.

CHAPTER 2

HOODOO AND HOLISM: A FRESH LOOK AT AFRICAN AMERICAN WELLNESS

B et you never thought you'd see these two words so solidly paired, but here they are—hoodoo and holism. When I want to convey the commonalities between earth-based spirituality forms and holistic health, my attention easily gravitates toward Hoodoo. Hoodoo, a type of ethno-medicine associated with African Americans, is the practice I know and the path I honor. I discuss it here to give another example of the way the soul is addressed and utilized in alternative spirituality.

Is Hoodoo a Religion?

No. Hoodoo is an eclectic group of ever-evolving, ever-changing folkloric practices. Hoodoo can be used to effect change in both a positive and a negative way. I chose to engage in its positive, healing aspects, and that is what you will find in this book.

Are Hoodoo and Voodoo the Same Thing?

No. Hoodoo is an American healing magickal tradition derived from practices in West Africa, whereas Vodou (the correct name for Voodoo) is an organized religion that comes to the United States from Haiti, though its roots, too, are in West Africa. Since my kin were from West Africa, Hoodoo is the primary Africanism that was passed down to me. The word "hoodoo," however, was seldom spoken by African Americans, who did not want to name or recognize this eclectic collection of African holdovers that endured and reminded us of the Middle Passage and slavery. The word "hoodoo" may have come from *juju,* which refers to African magick. The term "Hoodoo" is a useful container for the colorful and specific folkloric beliefs practiced by a wide range of believers including the Gullah people of Georgia and the Carolinas, black folk in major metropolitan areas, white folk of the Appalachians, and Native Americans.

Vodou, also spelled Vodoun or Vodun, is the correct name for the religion pejoratively (or through ignorance) called Voodoo. Though it derives from West African spirituality, it was influenced by Catholicism and, unlike Hoodoo, is an organized religion with priests. It is practiced mainly in the Creole areas of the United States and in the French-speaking Caribbean, notably Haiti. Vodou came to the mainland from Haiti, whereas many elements of Hoodoo came directly from Africa.

Other Forms of African Holistic Health

With immigration and migrations of freed slaves of North and South America, the growth of African derived religions (ADRs) and African traditional religions (ATRs) spread from the older cultural centers of Bahia, Brazil; Havana, Cuba; and Yorubaland, Africa to dynamic industrial centers such as New York City, Miami, Los Angeles, and Chicago.

Some of our traditional practices were transformed into systems strongly incorporating Catholicism. For example, the elaborate system of saints, priests, priestesses, deities, and ceremonies honored by Catholics is included in Santeria of Spanish-speaking countries and, as noted, the Vodou of French-speaking areas. Santeria, Shango, and Vodou are unique blends of Western and nonWestern religious rituals, ceremonies, prayers, invocations, and blessings, but they are also open to include the darker side of the spiritual world, including jinxes, curses, and hexes.

Hoodoo: An Eclectic Practice

Hoodoo is many things to many people. Yes, it has Native American and Appalachian influences, but its root is found in sub-Saharan Africa, and as such can be considered an African derived practice. In the Motherland, we were Africans of diverse language groups and tribes, involved in a unique lexicon of beliefs, lore, stories, and customs designed to help integrate us into a complex environment filled with plants, animals, elements, and a huge assortment of ancestors, deities, spirits, and deva.

With the advent of slavery, the physical bond with the Motherland was broken, but like seeds lifted from a ripe plant by wind, we found fertile ground in distant lands elsewhere. Our beliefs took root in slightly altered forms in the Americas. The freshly sown seedlings took hold most strongly in sunny climates reminiscent of the fair conditions in Africa. In the southern United States, Hoodoo took root in Alabama, Mississippi, Louisiana, Georgia, Florida, and North and South Carolina. Hoodoo was established during slavery using the plants available in the United States to treat our illnesses holistically, increase self-empowerment, and keep order.

In our building of Hoodoo, we borrowed from the ancient wisdom of others, including the Native Americans and the European Americans living among us. Between what we knew from Africa and what we learned in the New World, a tradition called Hoodoo slowly began and continues to evolve. Thus Hoodoo is multicultural and reflects strong links between various indigenous groups, Judeo-Christian faiths of the dominant cultures, and West African magickal and medicinal herbalism as well as some aspects of Hinduism, Zoroastrianism, and Buddhism.

Spiritual Term

Deva—In Hinduism and Buddhism, deva (pronounced day-vuh) is a goddess, god, "shining one," or divinity. According to Zoroastrianism, deva is one of an order of evil spirits. In New Age beliefs, a deva is often linked to a particular plant, natural object, or place and is not considered a negative or positive spirit but instead a source of knowledge.

Hoodoo involves the use of herbs, plants, roots, trees, animals, magnetic sand, minerals, and natural waters in conjunction with magickal amulets, chants, ceremonies, rituals, prayers, and hand-made power objects. Rather than placing power in the hands of religious leaders, by using these items, practitioners are empowered in Hoodoo to take control of their own fates.

Although Hoodoo, as some practitioners use it, may also embrace the darker side, many choose to practice it primarily as a healing tradition, designed to address and fix everyday problems, ensure justice, and move our people toward self-determination. This beautiful, though sometimes misconstrued, tradition is a unique merger of places, people, preferences, and beliefs.

Who's Attracted to Hoodoo?

Since it is not a religion, Hoodoo has always been practiced by a wide variety of people, regardless of ethnicity or religious affiliation. Its attractiveness lies in the fact that:

• It addresses both the mundane and sacred, physical and spiritual worlds.

• It is non-dogmatic.

• It is practical.

• It is non-exclusionary; all are welcome, including those with same-sex orientation, and, in fact, some of the work specifically addresses same-sex relationship.

The Work of Hoodoo

Primary

> Blessing the home.

> Keeping the domestic environment peaceful.

> Cleansing and banishing unwanted intrusions or bad vibes brought about by humans, animals, or spirits.

> Love draw (attracting loving partnerships).

> Money draw (attracting prosperity).

Other

> Partnership: gaining a life mate who loves unconditionally and doesn't cheat or abandon his/her spouse.

> The Good Life: gaining general health and happiness in life.

> Prophecy: predicting the future.

> Control Issues: controlling people when necessary and freeing oneself or others from undesired control.

> Hex/Unhex: using hexing to freeze negative intentions and unhexing to reverse negative magic.

> Luck: drawing luck in seeking employment, career advancement, or getting good grades in school.

> Prosperity and Abundance: winning money, lucky breaks, or the good fortune of success.

In short, Hoodoo is concerned with health, wealth, love, luck, and happiness—concerns to which many people can relate.

Employing Hoodoo in Holistic Health

Washes: Environmental washes to cleanse and renew the living environment or work space use blessed, magickal, and sacred waters such as lightning water, rainwater, seawater, and sweet (cologne) waters such as a type called Florida Water.

Baths with incantations: These baths bring cleansing, relaxation, and a variety of magickal herbs into the bathing experience, usually repeated on a set number of odd days (7, 9, 11, 13); ingredients and incantations also often utilize numerology and set patterns.

Candlemancy: Dressed candles (details to follow) used in specific colors and symbolic shapes and for a certain number of days or hours, provide space for enlightenment and focus on improvement of a situation.

Brooms: Also called besoms, brooms are natural and carry a great deal of symbolic and deity-related references from Africa. Brooms, especially when blessed, used correctly, and treated with specific washes to match the job, are great tools for restructuring the home or work space in a more positive light.

Minerals and magnetic sand: Minerals such as Dead Sea salt, chunks from various sources, pyrite dust, and magnetic sand all have specific purposes. Each of these substances might be added to the bathwater to lend it healing power for various reasons.

> Pyrite dust, also called fool's gold, is used in abundance and prosperity work.
> Magnetic sand is finely ground magnetic material sometimes called magnetic dust and used in Hoodoo baths and other rites and tricks to draw love, luck, and money to its user.
> Salt is used to alleviate pain, bring clarity, and cleanse the body, mind, and spirit. Salts have been used for cleansing and healing for thousands of years. They are enjoying a renewed interest by adherents of Feng Shui who use it in the same way as Hoodoo practitioners do. In these disparate practices, salt is placed on the floor and in corners of the room during spiritual cleansing.
> Crystals are used during bathing for curative and restorative properties.

Incense and smudging: Smoldering herbs and resins help charge a room (bringing positive, clear, clean vibrations to a space or object) but can also banish unwanted influences and generally clear a space. We retained this tradition from ancient Egypt. Numerous types of herbal incenses used have intriguing names, such as Crown of Success, Gris-Gris, Cast Off Evil, Kyphi, and Look Over Me. The incense is burned while chanting, singing, or praying.

Wearing amulets and talismans: This tradition is still carried on in sub-Saharan Africa. Wearing something as simple as garlic is known to keep away evil entities and illnesses. Knotted strings tied around the ankle are used for protection work. Amulets are typically placed inside a mojo bag, worn as a necklace, or, less frequently, worn as an anklet or bracelet.

Coins: Dimes and pennies have a particularly welcome place in positive Hoodoo magick.

Charged stones: Each of a wide variety of types has its own healing properties; the stones are worn on the person or carried in a mojo bag (see the following).

Symbolic animal parts: These are placed about the home or carried on the person to absorb evil; scarabs are an example.

Specially folded paper or parchment: Written on ritualistically with specific incantations, these are used for blessings, reflection, and protection.

Tricks and Mojo Bags

The method for achieving desired situations in Hoodoo is called "laying of tricks" and "fixing tricks," and is akin to European witchcraft spells and Romany charms. The charms used in Hoodoo are reminiscent of the African herbal bundles described in the previous chapter and are mostly referred to as *mojo bags*. The most common form of mojo bag, "a bag of tricks," employs herbs, minerals, and magnetic and other magickal ingredients. Other terms are as follows:

> **Nation sack**—magick bag once only found in the Memphis, Tennessee, area, where these bags grew into prominence in the early twentieth century and were used almost exclusively by women.

> **Gris-gris bag**—charm bag (another name for a mojo bag).

> **Mojo trick bag**—bag containing power objects for carrying out an intention.

> **Luck ball**—same as mojo trick bag, but smaller and can be shaped into a ball (rounded shape) when tied off.

> **Flannels**—refers to the material from which some mojo bags are made, typically red flannel.

LOVE DRAW NATION SACK

(for drawing love to the user)

Contains:

Male/female pair of blue lodestones

1 piece of orris root (Queen Elizabeth root)

3 dried red rosebuds

3 copper pennies

Personal items from the person you are drawing to you:

a photograph, lock of hair, button, soil from the bottom of shoes, or other things that contain his or her DNA

1 tablespoon powdered lemon verbena leaves

Handful crumbled rose petals

3 drops each of rose attar and lavender essential oil

2 drops angelica essential oil

Red flannel

Place first five ingredients on the red flannel and tie into a small sack. To make a scented feeding powder, blend together next four ingredients in the order given. Ladies keep this sack in your bra, under your garter belt, or under your belt. It must remain private and untouched by others! Feed weekly (feeding means to pay attention to and honor the bag by applying appropriate oils, minerals, powders, or herbs to enhance its power) on the day of Venus and Oshun—Friday. Think hard before doing this! You'll have difficulty getting rid of the man or woman you draw after working this trick!

How Can I Take "Bag of Tricks" Seriously?

Throughout magickal lore, there are words that seem caught in a time warp. "Magic" is one that is so specific to sleight of hand activities that most of us prefer the spelling "magick" to differentiate our magico-spiritual workings from stage play, smoke, and mirrors. Hoodoo does alter reality, objects, things, and situations as well as how we know them to exist; once upon a time, that would have been called by some "trickery." By and large in Hoodoo, we've held on to many colorful terms from the past but give them their own special meaning today, in the same manner as folks from other paths and practices have.

The phrases "my mojo" and "his/her bag of tricks" are often included in the song lyrics of traditional African American blues singers, particularly the legendary Muddy Waters (who is also called the Hoodoo Man). Unfortunately, the lyrics have been misinterpreted; "mojo" was interpreted as a metaphysical aura of sexual power or prowess, and the "trick bag" was misinterpreted as a metaphor for various forms of misleading behaviors.

In reality, a mojo and a bag of tricks are one and the same—a confluence of charms serving as an amulet for purposes ranging from attracting a lover and maintaining a relationship to drawing luck or attracting money. As noted, these bags are carried close to the person, usually on the thigh, in the bra, or in a special pouch under the clothing. If someone steals your mojo, they have stolen your special amulet that holds your hopes and dreams. The mojo is a personalized item that carries your personal energy; therefore, it is very dangerous and potentially fatal for it fall into the hands of another, especially if that person is a Hoodoo practitioner, witch, or conjurer.

The Use of Oils

In addition to the mojos, a wide variety of herb-based scented oils are employed in Hoodoo. Oils can be applied to the person, diffused in the air, set out in significant areas of the home, and used to dress candles. They are used to bring holistic health to the environment and to address the central concerns of Hoodoo. Whimsical names abound such as Van Van oil, Black Cat oil, Fast Luck oil, and Bend Over oil.

Dressing a Candle

Anointing or, as it is more commonly called, "dressing" is another way of feeding an object to bring its soul to life. This practice is used in Hoodoo to add extra strength to candles by uniting them with your intention, will, and energy. Dressing transforms the candle from a mundane object to a magically charged tool. Herbs and herb-infused oils are the best way of achieving a good dressing for jobs and tricks. To achieve a proper charge, one that is powered by the ancestors, deities, and spirits you honor, create your own oils, simply and inexpensively, using the following directions. Rest assured that with the ingredients gathered from the earth and sea, coupled with your focused intentions, your candles will be fully charged and capable of getting the job done right, for they will contain ashe (the collective powers of the universe).

Four Useful Candle Dressings

Place ingredients for your chosen dressing as follows in a sterilized bottle with a cork or nonreactive cap; store for four to six weeks to gain full potency. When ready, cover a piece of tin foil with an absorbent paper towel and lay the candles on the towel. Pour the herbal oil mixture on the candles and roll the candles in it. Use paper towel to blot away excess. Do this on Sunday or under New Moon for potency. Let the candle sit overnight before you light it.

Banishing: To 3 ounces safflower oil, add 3 drops each of essential oils of rose, geranium, lilac, bergamot, and frankincense. Place a frankincense tear (small lump), a piece of amber, and a few dried rose petals inside bottle.

Blessing: To 2 ounces of sunflower and 1 ounce light olive oil, add 2 drops each of essential oils of lavender and vetiver, an amethyst stone, and cinnamon chips to bottle.

Healing: To 2 ounces of sunflower and 1 ounce of light olive oil, add 4 drops of jasmine, 3 drops of attar of roses, 2 drops of frankincense, and 3 drops of myrrh. Keep a few tears of frankincense and myrrh in the bottle.

Holy: To 2 ounces safflower and 1 ounce of wheat germ oil, add 3 drops each of essential oils of frankincense, myrrh, cedar, and hyssop. Drop in a few flakes of gold leaf (or a small gold necklace) and a piece of hyssop herb.

Spiritual Tools of Hoodoo

Those who practice Hoodoo are likely to draw upon:

Crossroads: Sacred grounds on which you can make agreements with the spirits, place petitions, arbitrate, and send messages to the ancestors. This is a very special metaphysical space to Hoodoos because it represents the nexus of human world and ancestral and spiritual worlds.

Water: In Hoodoo, sweet waters (sweetly scented colognes) are also applied to the body and left in bowls to deter or attract spirits and humans.

Signs: Divination uses natural materials such as crystals, tea leaves, coffee grounds, animal bones, water gazing, crystal gazing, and seashells as oracles to predict the future.

Dreams: Dream interpretation, controlling dreams through lucid dreaming, and astral projection are important activities.

Spirits: Ancestral and natural spirits are acknowledged, invoked, and utilized for protection, predictions, healing, curses, and blessings. Hants are deterred.

Haven't Heard of Hants?

Deba—"Hant" (pronounced *hahnt)* is a mostly southern U.S. variant on the word "haunt." A hant is a supernatural creature akin to a ghost, which is usually undesirable and even downright scary.

Holistic Doctoring: A Path to Wellness

It's easy for many of us to understand holism, not just as a concept but also as a way of life. In black culture, even before we are
born, we may hear from the womb that we have "gotten on our
mother's nerves" or we absorb a litany of taboos piled upon our
poor mother's already strained frame, such as that certain foods
and animals will cause a hideous mark to come out on the child,
marring his or beauty. Contrariwise, we have internalized suggestions about blessings, soul-nourishing foods, life-affirming visitors,
and magickal signs, all before we even enter the world.

Even in the womb, it seems information courses through our
brains, permeating our soul with knowledge about the mind-body-
spirit connection. The information we absorb in the womb grows out
of a deeply held belief system. There is most definitely a connection
between mind, body, and spirit in sub-Saharan Africa, a triangular
connection that makes us whole and lends us ashe. When a segment
of our complex being, our wholeness, is impaired, it impacts *everything*.

The Neighborhood Guidance Counselor

A root doctor or other healer practicing ethno-medicine can
offer holistic guidance to help us restore our wholeness. This may
involve helping us interpret our dreams, visions, and suspected
visitations and assisting us in conjuration for our wellness. Our
most revered healers have always addressed the mental, physical,
and spiritual aspects of their client's situation, and minister to the
individual, family, parish, and community. Our holistic healers
are, as importantly, the shaman, priestess/priest, and root doctor.
"Holistic healer" is an umbrella term we use in the United States

for those whose work looks at the entire individual and his or her environment for clues that can lead to a complete diagnosis and positive prognosis.

Healer's Terms?

Natural Illness/Nature Cure–Naturally caused illnesses are biological and require conventional medicine, herbalism, chiropractic, acupuncture, or homeopathy, depending on the preference of the client. Spiritual/faith healing, including prayers and meditation, can assist in the healing process.

Unnatural Illness/Spiritual Cure–Unnatural illnesses can be sparked by hexing, chants, and conjuration (negative use of rootwork, spells, tricks, and dark rituals). Unnatural illness is typically treated with a combination of spiritual/faith-based ministering by a shaman, priestess, or rootworker that can include herbal cleansing, blessing, guided fasting, and guided meditation.

Complaints that may be shared with a root doctor or other holistic healer include (translation of each in *italics*):

> "She been touched in the head"—*may be referring to mental challenge, personality disorder, or other mental condition.*
> "They been gettin' on my nerves real good"—*an aggravated, anxious feeling that is overwhelming.*
> "Got itchy palms yet no money seems to be coming"—*superstition based; itchy palms equal incoming cash but could also spell out a physical complaint such as poor circulation.*

> "He just feels cold hearted"—*possible posttraumatic stress disorder; inability to connect to emotions or to others.*

> "She treat them kids too rough"—*another possible cry for help, this time with an abusive mother or other person in control of children.*

> "She too soft to deal with all them rough kids"—*a person possibly unsuited to child-rearing for mental, spiritual, or physical reasons who desperately needs help.*

> "She's just been worn down, don't want to talk to nobody"—*someone who is shutting down; may be suffering from a host of mind, body, or spirit issues (serious complaint).*

> "I'm afraid he's out of it for good"—*someone not dealing with life (similar to previous situation).*

> "Feeling faint all the time"—*could be a mental, physical, or spiritual complaint; though some would rush to a physical judgment, all possibilities for faintness should be considered.*

> "I'm just too cooped up"—*someone isolated; could be from an abusive situation or mental or spiritual disorder.*

> "That room needs a good airing out"—*a room that possibly needs spiritual cleansing, banishment, smudging, or opening up to the outside world.*

> "It's just messed up"—*a situation that seems hopeless; this may be a serious cry for help.*

Hoodoo Preservation

The most striking features of African based belief systems, such as belief in the collective power of nature, the employment of various deities, the power of prayer and self-determination, and shape Hoodoo, are shared in this book for the development and affirmation of personal strength, self-determination, connection to nature, awareness of the environment, and connection to our past.

Television, movies, and commerce tend to sap the vibrancy of authentic experience. In the first half of the twentieth century, Hollywood and unscrupulous businesses were captivated by the commercial and lucrative possibilities of Hoodoo. Sadly, the practice of Hoodoo went out of favor after it was commercialized and trivialized by the media and nonbelievers, but this creative practice of African American folklore deserves to be preserved and continued. Hoodoo is enjoying a huge resurgence due in part to Harry Middleton Hyatt's 5 volumes of *Hoodoo, Conjuration, Witchcraft, Rootwork.* There have been other contributions to this conversation by myself (my first book was *Sticks, Stones, Roots, and Bones: Hoodoo, Mojo, and Conjuring with Herbs*) and other interesting, qualified authors. Though I'd like to see the culture of Hoodoo as a holistic ethno-medicine preserved, it is clear that it, like everything else, evolves and changes with time.

A New Vision for Holistic Health

Hoodoo is a great tool in the arsenal of the holistic health worker that has been too often overlooked because of fear generated by the unscrupulous or the ignorant. There is a dark side to Hoodoo, including hexing and cursing, just as there is on many other paths and in well-known religions as well.

If you decide to focus on the positive aspects, you will find that in Hoodoo's colorful collection of beliefs and practices, there are workable cures and plausible solutions for aiding the whole person. In utilizing a holistic healing approach combined with Hoodoo's ethno-medicine, folklore, and cultural beliefs and practices, Hoodoo becomes an important part of your healer's medicine bag.

One of the more attractive features of Hoodoo is its built-in aspect of self-determination, a useful can-do spirit. The next chapter explores this theme in examining midwifery and some of the historic backdrop of African American healing as a soul medicine.

CHAPTER 3

IN MATTERS OF LIFE AND DEATH: IT BE BEST TUH HEAL OURSELVES

ou've probably heard quite a bit about Western herbalism and Chinese medicine, perhaps even some about Ayurveda, but perhaps not as much about African herbalism, which is often left out of the conversation. Part of the difficulty arises with semantics and the scarce use of the term "herbalist" and "herbalism" in reference to African American healers and their work. African American and Afro-Caribbean healers are called many different things, including Mothers, Secret Doctors, Root Doctors, and, simply, healers. Many African American healers are specialists engaged in various other professions that combine plant and folk remedies with other therapeutic activities to bring about wellness.

As we will explore later, some self-healers combine their work with a variety of activities including prayer, chanting, dancing, scripture, hand-played instruments, feathers, and hands-on energy work such as Reiki for greater efficacy. One of our most enduring and developed bodies of healing is found in midwifery. This chapter begins by exploring two different midwives, one from the antebellum south and one from contemporary Oregon. We go on to consider the personal testament of both myself and some of my close relatives in matters of how to live and how to die, raising important issues for us all.

Healer's Term

Reiki—The word *Reiki* is derived from two Japanese words, Rei, meaning "God's wisdom" or "The Higher Power," and *Ki,* which translates roughly as "life-force energy," what we call ashe in ATR and ADR. Reiki is a Japanese technique for alleviating and reducing stress while promoting relaxation. Sometimes, but not always, there is "laying on of hands" (a practice also utilized by African American healers) so that through touch, the Reiki (life-force energy/ashe) can be transmitted from one person to another. Reiki demonstrates the universality of healing and how close at times African alternative healing comes to Asian medicine.

Bearing Witness

Right from the beginning of life, our souls need proper nourishment. This may sound like a simple enough desire, but it is not always easy to fulfill, especially not during our lengthy history on these shores beginning as an enslaved people. Midwifery (the delivery of babies by midwives rather than doctors) has been a prominent African American holistic healing activity in the United States since our arrival in the United States in the 1600s. African American midwifery proliferated on plantations where African descended women delivered and tended to babies of white women and black.

Midwifery is an in-depth spiritual and pragmatic practice that envelops the mother, child, and entire family. According to midwife informants practicing in the early twentieth century, midwives not only delivered babies, they also discussed nutrition with their clients, tried to make the home environment as clean and comfortable as possible for the mother and child, and even served as homespun consuls, acting as liaisons between welfare organizations and the community.[1]

Doctorin' Ourselves

"In that time there was no hospital they[2] could go to have no baby. They didn't have clinics. They didn't have doctors. A doctor every now and then. When you call one, even if you call one today, he might come tomorrow. He might come tomorrow . . . I think that's one reason in the sight a God that midwives come about . . . it was the midwife or nothing."[3]

−Onnie Lee Logan

Onnie Lee's Story of Oppression, Healing, and Empowerment

Onnie Lee Logan, a lay midwife from a lineage of southern African American granny midwives, shares her observations, which include the social impetus for African Americans developing healing systems in her community. Onnie Lee was born in the early 1900s in rural Alabama. Onnie Lee's story, recorded by Professor Katherine Clark in *Motherwit: An Alabama Midwife's Story*, paints a scene of the relationship between whites and blacks in relation to health care and beyond in the following excerpts:

The white doctors at this time, let me tell you about the white doctors at this time. I don't think they paid too much attention to the black families then because the spirit of the white people then didn't go out for the black people. They didn't care. . . . They thought that we was—as they used to call us—animals. We were like animals. So they didn't have any feelin' for us.[4]

You know why the blacks avoided the white doctors? Because honey, they avoided the whites period. They be afraid to meet 'em. If a white person coming, they'll go away around him . . . and then they was treated so bad and so cold by the doctors. The doctors thought the black person was mostly too filthy for him to put his hands on. They talk to 'em just like they was a dog that didn't have human sense.[5]

In her memoir, Onnie Lee expresses the urgent need to develop African American midwifery within the black community. She found that without midwives there would be a dangerous shortage of health-care practitioners to deal with pregnancy, childbirth, and the post birthing experience. It is notable that she also reports on at least one male midwife in her family, indicating this was not an exclusively female occupation.

As Onnie's story unfolds, it is easy to see why natural therapy and home remedies, as well as those who knowledgably dispensed them, flourished in the black community.

Onnie Lee goes on to tell the sad story of her mother's stroke. It took about 26 hours for her mother to receive treatment. Eventually, her mother died from the complications of her stroke.

Shafia M. Monroe, Black Midwife

Shafia M. Monroe has a high profile as one of the most prominent black midwives in the United States. I mention her as a black midwife because her heritage is at the basis of her practice. Born in Massachusetts, she honors her Alabama roots, striving to keep alive the traditions of the granny midwife (like the work of Onnie Lee Logan). Shafia is the founder and coordinator of the annual International Black Midwives and Healers Conference. This international gathering brings together midwives, childbirth educators, doulas, lactation consultants, and others to discuss infant mortality prevention strategies, support networks, and professional development and education. As a birthing activist, Shafia organizes and motivates women to advocate for unique birthing experiences and positive birth outcomes.

Shafia, who has been practicing traditional midwifery for more than two decades, has stated, "I am committed to helping women understand African-centered midwifery. I hope to institutionalize the legacy of the black midwife. My style of holistic healing promotes breastfeeding as an important infant mortality preventative; this is woven into the model of care that I promote through practice and teaching." (From a personal e-mail interview.)

Midwifery is considered an alternative birthing practice—alternative to mainstream obstetrics in a hospital setting. Africans and Africans in the diaspora have historically depended on granny midwives because their services are cost-effective, convenient, and family-centered.

Today, outstanding African American midwives and birth activists such as Shafia have come into the limelight. Shafia founded the International Center for Traditional Childbearing (ICTC), a nonprofit grassroots organization focused on infant mortality prevention, pregnancy support, and midwife training. She helps provide birth companion/doula training, rites of passage for young women, and midwife training programs for those desiring these services. ICTC developed Sistah Care, a high school retention and mentoring program for female students interested in pursuing maternal and child health careers.

Doctorin' Ourselves

Shafia Monroe is president of Shafia Monroe Consulting/BIRTHING CHANGE. She is also an historian of African American Postpartum Foods. To learn more about traditional, southern-style granny midwifery, doulas, and reducing black infant mortality, visit *shafiamonroe.com*.

When the Past Is Too Present

I understand the need for midwifery, home doctoring, and natural medicine from personal experience. I empathize with Onnie Lee Logan and her story of her mother's death because I, too, felt the sting at the crossroads of racism and medicine. When I was growing up in rural South Jersey, we lived at the end of a dirt road in a segregated town. We were five miles from town, a customary distance at that time in that area of New Jersey for blacks and other people of color. We were also fifteen miles from the nearest hospital. My mother died from an embolism when she was in her early fifties. According to my family's account, she struggled for her life for almost half an hour as the family tried to help her in the best ways they knew, thinking it was simply an asthma attack, after which time the paramedics came and tried to revive her, to no avail. We were stunned because my mother regularly saw her family physician, who had done X-rays on her prior to her death. It was difficult to understand how such a condition like a blood clot went undetected and ended up killing her even after an extensive battery of X-rays.

Remembering the Tuskegee Syphilis Study, or the Investigation into "Bad Blood"

For generations, there was not just the fear of being unable to get treatment in time because of unforgiving geography or uncaring doctors. There was, and to some extent still is, suspicion about what the white doctors might do to harm the patient. Indeed, rumors of deadly medicines being given as experiments abound in our culture. These might be dismissed as paranoid conspiracy theory were it not for the well-documented case of African American men with syphilis given no treatment.

The grim experiment on these men is summarized by Loudell Snow, author and professor of anthropology, human development, and pediatrics: "It is best to keep in mind the infamous Tuskegee Syphilis Study before deriding such belief.[6] The Public Health Service funded the study, which began in 1932 and continued until 1972. It included a large sample of poor African American men infected with syphilis; they were not educated about the true nature of their disease but were told that they had 'bad blood,'[7] the folk term . . . covering a variety of problems. And they were left untreated so that researchers might have an opportunity to observe the natural course of the disease until 'end point,' that is, autopsy."[8]

The large sample of black men numbered four hundred. As though deception were not bad enough for the men involved, their families were directly affected. An estimated fifty women, wives and mates of the infected men, contracted syphilis from them, and seventeen children and two grandchildren were born with congenital syphilis.[9]

Living and Dying on Our Own Terms

Cancer took many members of my family, including my beloved father, my grandmother (his mother), and her sister (my great-aunt). My father and grandmother were great believers in herbal/natural remedies and instilled these beliefs in me. My grandmother did not seek conventional medical treatment or tests until she was at the end stages of her cancer. I remember she grew fond of fresh juices like papaya and banana and developed a strong predilection for licorice.

I recall stories indicating that there was a great deal of fear about cutting or surgeries at the hands of doctors because it was believed that the act of cutting and removal of tissue itself would accelerate the illness.

My father and grandmother lived at home with their cancer, drinking vegetable and fruit juices, taking tonics, minerals, and other natural supplements, many of which I developed for my father to augment his mainstream care. The two did their best to go about a "normal life" at home as much as possible and eventually combined conventional medicine with natural medicines to alleviate their symptoms. Meanwhile, until the end of their lives on this Earth, they sought alternative treatments that could offer relief if not a cure.

Licorice

True licorice sticks (not the candy) were tied to the necks of some enslaved Africans during the journey across the Atlantic to quell stomachache and anxiety. It is believed to be how the seeds of the plants were transported and later established in the United States. Licorice is still used in the black community for stomach pains.

Art as Therapy

In black culture, regular people without a specialized title such as an art, dance, movement, or music therapist have long understood the transformative powers and therapeutic abilities of talking drums, which we call *djembe* (or *jembe*), spiritual dancing, shuffling, clapping, tapping, humming, whistling, singing, chanting, shouting, and making art. In Africa and the African diaspora, the marriage of art and healing isn't called music, dance, or art therapy; it is considered part of community ritual and ceremony employed during life passages and uneasy transitions. In fact, rather than gossiping or questioning one another at family get-togethers, the most rewarding activity can be spontaneous group dance. This puts us in touch with our individual souls and those of our family members.

Arts like herbalism have been used therapeutically, often with a specific purpose tied to the Wheel of the Year, a pre-Christian schedule of the year that includes many astrological and agrarian observations, honored through ritual and ceremony, various rites of passage, holidays, or other understood psychospiritual contexts reflective of faith.

Drumming

Drumming can lend power and purpose to your life journey. Drumming is useful for every passage: birthing, coming of age rituals, weddings, easing the journey of the seriously ill, and as an addition to funerary rites. It is a creative outlet and distraction. Drumming provides mental and physical exercise while at the same time transporting the drummer to another dimension in space.

Your Drumming Circle

Setting up a drumming circle in your home is easy. Here's how to do it.

1. Contact your local African drummer, Afrocentric bookstore/ resource, or music school or search your cultural newspaper.
2. Seek a skilled and patient drummer as the leader.
3. Look for appropriate drums that are suitable to your body size and weight and are attractive; E-bay is a decent source, as is 10,000 Villages (a fair-trade international store) or an Afrocentric store in your community.
4. Gather together a group of your friends or simply form the circle from your family.
5. Decide how frequently to meet and how much to pay the leader. This is money well spent!

When the Healer Needs Healing

At times, some of the people most in need of healing are healers themselves. Treating my uncle through a difficult illness and passage taught me valuable lessons about healing a healer.

My uncle, of whom I speak frequently, was my father's younger brother. He did what my father and my grandmother did to deal with serious illness, though he had HIV rather than cancer. He took whole foods as medicines, especially soul foods such as collard greens, yams, beans, and rice, herbal and mineral supplements, and sought out the assistance of a fellow babalawo.

While my father delved deeper into Christianity as his years advanced, my uncle during his life's journey went deep into the spiritual dimension customary in various ATRs.

My uncle lived with HIV for fourteen years before it developed into AIDS. He was very reluctant to take conventional medicines, fearing that HIV/AIDS was the creation of scientists who wanted to wipe out the black race. With that belief firmly rooted, he could not trust Western medicine.

Instead, he performed and participated in rituals and ceremonies, and he used djembe and congas therapeutically. He was a former drummer for the progressive group Sun Ra during the 1960s and 1970s. I credit these alternative therapies with extending his life and enhancing its quality during his illness.

Healing and Health Equal Activism

Whereas Onnie Lee's story tells of the early to mid-1800s, my uncle and father carried similar beliefs to hers into the twenty-first century. The fact that blacks were forced to live so far from town only added to the already well-placed suspicions of the mainstream medical establishment. My father, I am sad to say, died in 2004 of cancer, and his brother died a few years before him of AIDS.

For my uncle and many African Americans who choose natural remedies and complementary therapies over conventional medicine and mainstream doctors, the choice reflects a quest for self-determination and empowerment. Engaging in CAM (comple-mentary and alternative medicine) is frequently connected to activ-ism in the black community. It is notable that my uncle, a Black Power and Civil Rights activist in the 1960s and 1970s, was like many African Americans who became involved with wellness, holistic health, and natural remedies.

CAM and Integrative Health

Integrative health seeks to combine conventional med-icine with CAM and alternative health care (CAHC). CAM, an acronym that stands for complementary and alternative medicine, covers a broad spectrum of healing ways not considered conventional medicine. The focus of integrative health is on wellness and prevention. It is a people-centered medicine that considers mind, body, and spirit in health and healing.

Becoming a Healer

Whereas plantation owners and their families might have been content to interact with the field and forest from afar, on horseback, or through a screened-in porch, enslaved men and women, by the very nature of their work, witnessed and experienced their environs at eye level, creating a myopic vision and infinite understanding of their environment and its plants and natural resources.

The effective African American healer today needs to be involved with her community, whether that means her household, relatives, friends, neighborhood, or village at large. The purpose is to know the area's indigenous healing plants, which to use and which to avoid, and how to match medicines available to the needs within that community.

Before beginning outreach as an herbalist or midwife, the effective healer needs cultivated knowledge (usually gained empirically), empathy for her clients, and understanding gleaned from a shared history. Healing begins with a sincere desire from the heart, which is why many consider it a divine calling. We may not have ample monetary resources, but we can always count on creativity as one of the modes of self-healing, utilizing art, music, dance, and song in the way of our ancestors.

CHAPTER 4

RED: THE STRENGTH AND POWER OF BLOOD

Ⅰn many indigenous cultures where African traditional religions (ATRs) and African derived religions (ADRs) are practiced, animals are sacrificed, and the blood, a most precious gift, is submitted to the spirits to ask for their blessings and show appreciation. The mystical quality of blood is a unifying element in our stories about health, what it means to be whole and sound in body and soul. In the African diaspora, vegetables, fruits, and herbs that resemble blood when prepared are utilized medicinally, sometimes even as cure-alls. This is because of an underlying belief in the mystery, strength, and power of blood and the special symbolism of the color red. After all, as long as our blood flows, we are alive; when it stops, we have passed over into the great beyond. This carries over to rituals of life and death and also impacts health.

This chapter is divided into five parts. In the first part, we explore the notion of the "heart-soul" *(ab)* in its multiple manifestations, as well as the concept of good and bad blood, noticing how this concept affects healing practices in the diaspora. In the second part, we examine the power of beets for heart and blood health. The third part looks at *pupa* medicines; *pupa* is a Yoruban medicine term for herbs, vegetables, and fruits of specific symbolic relation to the blood. The fourth part of this chapter details a cache of herbs used to ease rites of passage (specifically the passing of blood by women). Finally, part five looks at warrior herbs.

Part I—Ab: The Heart-Soul

In Egyptian medicine, heart was *ab*, or "the heart-soul." The seven birth goddesses called the Hathors or Holy Midwives are associated with the seven heavenly spheres. The Hathors gave each Egyptian seven souls at birth, one of which is the soul heart. It was considered the most important of the seven souls.[1]

Judicious goddess Ma'at weighed the ab against her feather of truth to see if it was too heavy with sin, and Osiris's mummy received an ab in the form of an amulet made from a red stone to ensure vitality. Eventually, *ab* came to mean both "offering" and "heart." The hieroglyph for *ab* was a dancing figure, so it also became associated with the mystical dance of life going on inside the body: the heartbeat.

Bantu witches remember the Egyptian way. They cast a death spell by symbolically eating the heart of an intended victim to consume his/her "heart-life." Egyptian ideas of the heart, passed down into African diasporic healing, hold that the heart is the seat of the self. This is why the terms "heavy heart" or "lighthearted" reflect a mental state and "heartache" or "heartbreak" are used to describe longing for a loved one.[2]

Development of Blood and Heart Medicine

The healing practiced by African American heart healers and the Mother Healers of Jamaica is, not surprisingly, quite similar. They synchronize the four elements and the four humors, a system attributed to the ancient Greek Hippocrates, based on medical knowledge learned from the ancient Egyptians (and presumably from the nearby early African civilizations such as Nubia, Kush, and

Axum that served as cultural crossroads) whose culture informs all of Africa's cultures.

According to the four humors system, the body is filled with four basic substances, called humors, which are balanced when we are well. Diseases and disabilities result from an excess or deficit of one of these four humors. The four humors are:

1. Black bile
2. Yellow bile
3. Phlegm
4. Blood

It was believed that each humor fluctuates with time, diet, and activity. When someone suffered from too much of one humor or an imbalance of the humors, that person's psychological and physical state was thought to be impacted. The four humors were closely related to the four elements:

1. Earth (black bile)
2. Fire (yellow bile)
3. Water (phlegm)
4. Air (all four are represented by the blood through air)

In time, blood became the primary focus of the Hippocratic humoral theory and was considered to be a primary health concern. This complements the African belief, based on Egyptian philosophy, that the blood is an organ and that balanced blood, neither too hot nor too cool, is essential to good health.

Jamaican Blood Works

When I mention diasporic heart practice, a Caribbean country that comes immediately to mind is Jamaica, the place where many of us here in America were "seasoned" before our U.S. enslavement.

SPIRITUAL HEART HEALER'S MEDICINE KIT

Here are Western herbs for dealing with heart ailments of various kinds:

angelica	hawthorn
arnica	horse chestnut
balm	kola tree
barberry	lady's mantle
bear's foot	lily of the valley
bear's garlic	Mexican tea
bennet	milfoil
betony	mistletoe
bistort	motherwort
black hellebore	mugwort
bloodroot	oat
blue cohosh	onion
blue vervain	pasque flower
borage	primrose
buttercup	rosemary
calendula	rue
cayenne	St. John's wort
cowslip	shepherd's purse
cucumber	silverweed
Euro-mistletoe	strawberry bush
foxglove	valerian
garden violet	Virginia snakeroot
garlic	wahoo
green hellebore	wormseed

Heart and blood working is an evident preoccupation in the work of the Mother Healers of Jamaica whose very name shows that their work is imbued with love; they are healers with heart and they employ spirit heavily to accomplish their work.

The traditional forms of African-Jamaican medicine are diverse. The vein that runs through it is how to treat the blood: how to strengthen it and balance it, so it is neither too sweet nor too bitter, and how to build it up and cool it down. This is a concern that began in the Motherland and is addressed by folk medicine in various locations throughout the African diaspora today.

Diasporic Blood Lore

Jamaica–Tonics and purifiers are taken to keep the blood strong, thick, and circulating properly.

Trinidad, Puerto Rico, and Guadeloupe–There is more concentration on cooling the blood so it is not too hot, whereas in Jamaica the focus is on reducing sweetness.[3]

Rastafarians–They avoid foods that are not raised organically. Foods treated with pesticides and fertilizers are deemed too hot; since chemicals can actually burn plants, it is thought that those plants will also heat up the blood.

Part II—Beets: Making the Body Rich and Strong

Mothers have many ways of encouraging their children to eat a wholesome diet. I remember my mother could wax for hours on end about beets. She would say things like "Beets give you strength, vitality, and strong blood," and then later, "Beets are sexy." Encouraged by my mother's seemingly unending enthusiasm for them and knowing that this was something passed down to her by her mother and her mother before her, I ate beets regularly (though, to my young opinion, they did not taste all that great).

Researchers have investigated the health-promoting qualities of beets. This is what they found:

Red *is* healthy: Phytonutrients called betacyanins give beets their red color.

Antioxidant rich: In a clinical trial of antioxidants present in fruits and vegetables capable of reducing the damage caused by oxygen radicals, researchers found beets to contain 840 of the 3,500 ORAC (oxygen radical absorbance capacity) units needed per day.[5] Beets are in the top ten antioxidant vegetables and legumes category. The other red ones in the group are red bell pepper and kidney beans. As for red fruit, watermelon is ranked high, as are red grapes, strawberries, raspberries, and cranberries.

Betain: Beets contain betain, found in only a few other foods. It is a colorless crystal that plays a role in detoxifying homocysteine, a troublesome amino acid implicated in heart disease. Beets also contain salicylic acid, a close relative of aspirin (acetylsalicylic acid) and have some of the anti-inflammatory qualities of aspirin. It would seem that our mothers were not off track with their color-equals-good-health theory, after all.[6]

A threat to cancer—*Good ole red beet:* In the 1950s, Hungarian doctor Alexander Ferenczi treated inoperable cancer patients with beets. They ate a diet high in organic beet juice and raw beets. Twenty-two of the twenty-three patients had some degree of improvement, including tumor regression and weight gain. Dr.

Govind Kapadia, professor of biomedicinal chemistry at the historically black college Howard University, conducted experiments that found that beet extract profoundly inhibits skin, lung, and liver tumors in mice.[7]

Aids addiction cessation: Beet greens (the tops) are also used to fight addiction to cigarettes.[8]

Part III—Pupa Medicines

In the Yoruba cosmology, red, called *pupa*, includes the colors yellow, brown, and red. Red is the color of the earth and the sky is white.[9] The pupa medicines are fruits, vegetables, and herbs that are red, yellow, or orange in color. From both a traditional African medical standpoint and a Western one, they have particularly strong medicine. The following are a few examples.

Henna *(Lawsonia inermis)*

Though henna is discussed at length in a later chapter, it also belongs in this conversation because its renowned red dye plays an important role in West African healing. Henna is used to stop bleeding.[10] The leaves and fruit are used to bring on absent periods (amenorrhea).[11] Hina, the plant oil combined with sandalwood, is used as an aphrodisiac, particularly by men in North and East Africa.

Rose *(Rosa spp.)*

Roses were first grown in the Middle East in Persia and spread through Saudi Arabia, North Africa, and then to Europe. They also grow well in the United States. *Rosa damascena*, one of the most fragrant types, is used to make perfumes and rosewater. It grows well in Morocco and is cultivated in North Africa. In North Africa, rose is used to treat matters of the heart spiritually by calming irritability and anxiety. When mixed with oil, rose petals create a hemostatic (stems bleeding) powder that can be used to treat nasal, auricular, and blennorrhagial infections.

In temperate zones, rose hips make a vibrant red color in the otherwise drab winter landscape. When infused in very hot water, rose hips release a deep burgundy tea. Rose hip tea is high in vitamins C, A, D, and B complex as well as bioflavonoids. The bioflavonoids allow our bodies to more readily absorb the vitamin C. Rose hips also contain minerals: calcium, iron, silicon, selenium, manganese, magnesium, phosphorus, potassium, and zinc. As a tea, it can be served hot or cold—both ways work beautifully—to build immunity, strength, and vitality. Rose hips contain antioxidants and act as an antidepressant. Rose hip tea helps scavenge free radicals; it is a tension tamer, which soothes the nerves; and helps regulate the circulation. Also, it is considered a recovery tonic, spring tonic, and system cleanser.

Rooibos or Rooibosch (Aspalathus linearis)

Rooibos is called by many names, such as "bossie." It grows exclusively in the Clanwilliam district of the Western Cape of South Africa,[12] where the age-old tradition of wildcrafting (harvesting the herb from wild rather than cultivated spaces) the organic herb continues. It is truly a remarkable red medicine. Rooibos has fifty times more antioxidants than green tea, and it contains a free radical damage scavenger, superoxide dismutase (SOD), which helps keep fat from turning into harmful lipid peroxides.

Quercetin, a phytonutrient called a flavonol, brings the greatest gift to our blood, lending the tea the ability to prevent hemorrhaging, increase circulation, build capillary strength, and fight infections.[13] Rooibos mineral counts, per 200 milliliters tea, illustrate its overall health benefits: calcium (1.09 mg), copper (0.07 mg), fluoride (0.22 mg), iron (0.07 mg), manganese (0.04 mg), magnesium (1.57 mg), sodium (6.16 mg), and zinc (0.04).[14]

Rose Madder *(Rubia tinctorum L.)*

Madder root is grown in North Africa, from Libya to Morocco. The root of rose madder, or "madder" as it is also called, makes an exquisite dye used in fine arts and crafts. The dye is also very useful for hair; an infusion stains hair a deep claret red. The roots are boiled for a tea to treat emmenagogue (promotes menstruation). The stems and leaves are used to treat hypertension. The powdered plant is useful in dressing contusions and wounds. Madder is helpful for all blood diseases and is also used as an aphrodisiac.[15]

Part IV—Rites of Passage

Women see their blood vividly from the onset of menarche through menopause. Each month we see, flowing from between our legs, evidence of the power and mystery of creation. To the Yoruba medicine people, this is the hidden secret of red manifested by the body. Menstrual blood is used in cleansing, blessing, health, and deity invocation rituals. It is not considered a dead or useless substance, as it tends to be from a Western biomedical view. In Yoruba medicine, ideal menstruation, in color, duration, texture, and scent, is called *pupa daa daa* (okay red) and it contains a great deal of information about a woman's overall health.[16] Not surprisingly, there is a cache of herbs to address various elements of our blood passage.

Nettle *(Urtica dioica)*

This is a mineral-rich, all-around body strengthener, blood cleanser, and detoxicant. Where nettle grows, from Egypt to Morocco, it is used as an aphrodisiac and antihemorrhagic, and in the treatment of dysmenorrhea (pain during menses), nosebleeds, and eczema.

Several types of nettle also grow in South Africa and are used medicinally, such as bush stinging nettle *(U. urens)*, which is also called bosbrandnetel. In this region, the powdered leaves are stuffed in the nose to stem nosebleeds and are also used for blood disorders. River nettle or riviernetel *(Laportea peduncularis)* is a South African native nettle that is used in much the same way.

Raspberry *(Rubus idaeus)*

In the wisewoman way, raspberry leaf is considered one of the most important plants to a woman's reproductive development. Raspberry, a member of the rose family, contains fragrine, an alkaloid that strengthens the uterus, helps produce effective con-

---

Red Fruit as Medicine

In addition to the leaf, the fruit of the raspberry is recommended for its abundance of red medicines and antioxidants to promote good health, vitality, and strength. For the same reason, seasonal, organic strawberries, cherries, red grapes, and cranberries are also recommended.

---

tractions during labor, tones the womb, and expels the afterbirth. In cases of miscarriage or abortion, raspberry leaf is used to help regain strength, vitality, and the tone of the uterus. I recommend that young girls begin drinking raspberry leaf tea near the onset of their first period and continue to use it on a monthly basis throughout their lives.

Black Cohosh (Cimicifuga racemosa)

This herb is also called rattleroot and black snakeroot. It is a traditional women's healing herb, appreciated for its ability to assist with PMS, menstrual discomfort, and menopause. Black cohosh is native to eastern North America and is found in rich shady forests from Maine north to Ontario, and from Wisconsin south to Georgia and Missouri. Black cohosh is the largest selling herbal supplement and, as its folk names of rattleroot and black snakeroot indicate, it carries snake symbolism. According to the Expanded Commission E, a group that researches herbs and verifies their efficacy as herbal medicine in evidence-based studies, black cohosh binds weakly with estrogen and influences the endocrine regulatory system, affecting it in similar ways to estriol, one of the milder endogenous estrogens. As a popular herb, black cohosh has gone through numerous scientific tests for its efficacy. The Commission E now approves the use of black cohosh root for PMS, dysmenorrhea, and menopause. One of its constituents, acteina, is being evaluated for the treatment of peripheral arterial disease. (A side effect is occasional gas. Not recommended during pregnancy or lactation.)

Black Cohosh Tea

Decoct 40 mg (about a cup and a half) of cut rhizome and root in 2 cups simmering water. Drink this amount daily.

Motherwort *(Leonurus cardiaca)*

A native of Europe, motherwort, meaning "mother herb," is known to be an herb of the blood. The stem shoots straight up, and is both strong and thick. There are three large three-lobed leaves. Motherwort helps maintain heart health and is beneficial to women's reproductive systems. It is calming and soothing to the nerves. This mothering tea helps the woman's reproductive system by assisting with some of the discomforts that may arise with menses and menopause.

The word *cardiaca,* part of the Latin name for motherwort, demonstrates that it has a long history as a heart tonic herb. The herb contains calcium chloride, which calms the heart and eases palpitations. Motherwort is a great stabilizing herb that stops internal tremors. The Commission E recommends motherwort for heart palpitations that result from anxiety attacks or other nervous complaints.

Historically, motherwort has been a medicine to treat heart weakness, absence of periods, and cardiac symptoms associated with nerves.

Actions: cardiac tonic, antispasmodic, nervine, diaphoretic, uterine stimulant, sedative, emmenagogue, carminative

Contains: vitamin A, alkaloids, bufanolide, bitter glycosides, tannins

Recommendation: utilize the stem, leaves, and flower as a decoction or tea; harvest during the plant's blooming season.

Part V—Warrior Herbs

Blood red is associated with life, yet it is also connected to violence and death. In the Yoruba cosmology, Ogun is the Orisha (god) of war, weaponry, metals, and strength, and is connected to the heart region. His herbs include motherwort, which we just discussed, garlic, bloodwort, and hawthorn, which we explore in this section, along with yarrow, all of which are useful for the wounds, bleeding, and other afflictions of warriors.

— SP☼TLIGHT—

Garlic *(Allium sativum)*

Garlic, a bulb with multiple wedge-shaped cloves and a papery white or sometimes purplish skin, is beloved in African stews and curries, as well as dishes from North Africa and the Caribbean. Like honey, pungent garlic is used as a spice to balance the sweet fruits used in cooking.[17]

In South Africa, wild garlic *(Tulbaghia violacea)* grows on the Eastern Cape and Natal. Its leaves are eaten to strengthen the body and it is rubbed on the forehead for sinus pain. *T. alliacea*, African wild garlic, grows from Cape Province northward to Natal, and the Transvaal west to Botswana. The roots are boiled and used in a bath to treat rheumatism and cure paralysis.[18]

In North Africa, garlic is called *thoum* or *toum* in Arabic. It is used as an antidote for many different kinds of poisons and as an antibacterial, stimulant, tonic, and antiseptic. Garlic is inserted as a suppository to treat hemorrhoids and it is also used as an animal medicine.[19]

Garlic is the health warrior of all warriors; no wonder it is the *ewe* (herb) that traditionally represents Ogun. Garlic is a broad-spectrum antibiotic that combats bacteria, intestinal parasites, and viruses. It contains more than two hundred compounds, including at least twenty germ killers, antioxidants, and a dozen anti-inflammatory chemicals. In high doses, it has cured encephalitis (inflammation of the brain). Among garlic's many compounds are the organosulfur compounds, which are also found in onions, leeks, and chives. These compounds may be responsible for garlic's antibacterial and antifungal abilities as well as the quality of slowing cholesterol synthesis, lowering blood pressure, reducing atherosclerosis, and inhibiting platelet aggregation.

African American Garlic Protection

In Hoodoo and similar practices, 4 Thieves Vinegar, a garlic-imbued elixir, is a popular potion to ward off evil. Bulbs of garlic hung over the door ward off burglars, malintent, and illness.

Granny healers and treaters,[20] two types of African American natural/spiritual healers from different parts of Louisiana, use garlic as a protective amulet. It is placed in a protective pouch constructed of a piece of symbolic cloth. The cloth is sealed and strung on string, which is carefully knotted in a manner that has been passed down for generations. The amulet is then hung around the waist of children as a vermifuge (medicine that expels intestinal worms) or around adults to protect from illness. Garlic, considered a holy herb, is used to curb evil and bring about goodness, which in turn yields health and well-being. This type of amulet medicine is practiced traditionally in Africa, the Caribbean, and various parts of North and South America, most notably Louisiana.[21]

Garlic Consumption Tips

> After chopping or mincing garlic, let it sit for fifteen minutes before using; this enables the release of the beneficial organosulfur compounds.

> A Bahamian weight-loss formula suggests adding three to four minced garlic cloves to one gallon of spring water. Start drinking it first thing in the morning to curb your appetite.

> Combining garlic with selenium-rich foods such as fish and whole grains also boosts benefits.

> Raw garlic is recommended for fighting bacteria.

> Cooked garlic is recommended for blood thinning and cardio-protective qualities. Cooking releases antithrombotic ajoene contained in garlic.

> In cases of cancer, raw, pickled, or aged garlic might be better than cooked.[22]

Bloodwort *(Lachnanthes caroliniana)*

Also called bistort, this herb is used to stop hemorrhaging. Applied to a wound as a powder, it is said to stop bleeding. Bloodwort is an alternative astringent, diuretic, and styptic. To use bloodwort, add two teaspoons of rootstock to one cup of water. Boil five to ten minutes and drink only one cup per day.

— SP✵TLIGHT—

Hawthorn *(Crataegus oxyacantha, C. monogyna)*

Hawthorn, also called sacred herb, is a powerhouse. No wonder that it, too, is associated with the warrior Orisha Ogun. Hawthorn, common in Asia, Europe, and North Africa, is a heart tonic that enhances blood circulation and improves uptake of oxygen; it also helps regulate the heart rate, stabilize blood pressure, increase relaxation, and reduce stress on the nerves.

Contrary to popular belief, the Commission E recommends the leaves and flowers of hawthorn rather than its berries for maximum health-producing benefits.[23] The Commission E reports that hawthorn, used in conjunction with cardiovascular medications such as digitalis and oubain, increases recovery time from cardiovascular disease and helps patients better tolerate the medications.[24]

Hawthorn contains vitamins A, B complex, and C; the minerals sodium, silicon, iron, manganese, potassium, phosphorus, and selenium; and saponins, glycosides, flavonoids, tannin, and procyanidins. It is a cardiovascular tonic, hypertensive, vasodilator, relaxant, astringent, antispasmodic, and diuretic.

Yarrow (Achillea millefolium)

Yarrow has a tradition as a warrior's herb. Women of the wise-woman way (herbal feminine-centered healers) utilize it as an over-all toner and systemic strengthener. It has also traditionally been used to treat high blood pressure. It can help stop bleeding, tone the pelvic muscles in the treatment of uterine disorders, relieve tension or pressure on the lower body, and regulate and reduce heavy periods or feelings of uterine fullness. Yarrow works with the veins as an anti-inflammatory to reduce vascular appearance. It is an antiseptic yet can be used as a poultice on varicose veins. Yarrow sitz baths are recommended for hemorrhoids. Wounds are cleaned and the cuts seal quickly with the encouragement of yarrow tea or poultice. Soothing yarrow is also useful in treating burn injuries, ulcers, and inflamed skin. The silica it contains repairs damaged skin.

My favorite yarrow poultice is simple: Chew fresh clean yarrow to moisten it with saliva; apply to nosebleed, cut, or wound.

> **Parts used:** plant and flowers
>
> **Contains:** vitamins A, B complex, C, and E, bioflavonoids, minerals, amino acids, sterols, coumarins, saponins, salicyclic acid, and more.[25]

Heart-Soul Summary

The heart-soul is such a multileveled deep subject that it needs to be discussed in layers. The heart is a real organ within our bodies, but it is also a symbolic object that determines our holistic health. This heart section began with ancient Egyptian ideas about the blood as an organ and how that information filtered through the Greek physicians and eventually trickled down to us.

Heart means so much in the African community—bravery, tenderness, strength, courage, love, and a certain "rightness" that leads to overall balance. Heart is often aligned with soul as well. My goal here has been to present some of the complexity of heart and soul as it existed in Africa and has manifested in the United States because understanding ab allows us to build an earth-wise lifestyle geared toward wellness.

Chapter 5 continues the discussion of herbalism, focused around the Yoruba deity of herbal medicines, Osayin, and his gifts to us.

AS IT IS ABOVE: OSAYIN'S GIFT BASKET

ccording to African griots (storytellers), there was an Orisha (deity) named Osayin. Unlike most of the other Orishas who were birthed by Orisha parents, Osayin sprang forth from the womb of Mother Earth, like a seedling. Because of his affinity for nature, and trees in particular, he stayed hidden within the forests, where he learned all there is to know about plants.

Like most African deities throughout the continent, from Egypt to the most southern parts of Africa, this deity was imperfect, making him relate well to humans and their weaknesses. For example, Osayin was extremely possessive of his charges, which happened to have been all the herbs from the tops of the forest to the farm and down to the sea. His familiar chant was *"Ewe O, Ewe O!"* ("My plants, my plants!" in Yoruba).[1]

The greatest herbalist in the world didn't want his shine reduced by other Orishas that might share his knowledge. Osayin thus hid the knowledge of medicines and how to speak their language in the tops of trees, in a *guiro*, also called a calabash, symbolic of all African healing plants.

The other Orishas of the world were unhappy about what Osayin had done, and he was punished quite severely. Oya, Orisha of weather and changes, stirred up a mighty wind at the urging of several other Orishas, and down to Earth came Osayin's hidden herbal knowledge.

Osayin is still around today, and many worship him. He represents an open-minded vision similar to Hoodoo's acceptance of all people, from all different walks of life and orientations. Osayin is a hermaphrodite and his image appears in beautiful blues and greens. He has a tiny ear that hears extremely well and a gigantic ear that cannot hear at all. He also has one bad arm and leg, so he limps around painfully. His voice is shrill to the ears. He is comfortable both in the water and in the forest and adores shiny things. Osayin's gift basket of herbal knowledge still stems from the calabash—as I said, a symbolic plant in itself, with many uses. People of African descent have long relished the calabash's closest relative, the melon. Osayin's story begins with the calabash but includes other related foods of the soul from Africa and many that we enjoy here in the New World.

Spiritual Term

Orisha—Practitioners of Ifa believe numerous Orishas (deities) populate the world. Today, there is mainstream discussion and appreciation of about twelve Orishas, but there are actually nearly five hundred. Intimate contact with an Orisha can bring about dramatic changes difficult for science to explain. Some other spiritual paths liken Orishas to the gods and goddesses found elsewhere around the world. In Catholicism, Saint Benito, Saint Jerome, and Saint Joseph are akin to Osayin.[2]

"As it is above" makes commentary on the once rarified knowledge of herbs that is now increasingly available to everyone. This chapter unravels the many ways we can utilize Osayin's gift basket of soul food for optimal holistic health. The calabash family is extensive, nutritious, and useful for many contemporary ills. Osayin's symbolic color, green, affords the opportunity to discuss a wholesome class of foods once deemed lowly. The conversation flows like healthy blood through the thriving body of knowledge, ending, in this chapter, with honey.

Family Cucurbitaceae

It is easy to see the wonder and fear with which Osayin is viewed. Many of the life-sustaining herbs of Africa and the Black Atlantic are in Osayin's family—Cucurbitaceae. This family of plants includes:

Cucumis (cucumber and melon)

Momordica charantia (African cucumber)

Cucurbita (pumpkin and marrows)

Citrullus vulgaris (watermelon)

Luffa cylindrical (vegetable sponge)

Lagenaria (gourd)

The Four Great Cold Seeds of the old *materia medica* were:
1. Seeds of the pumpkin
2. Seeds of the gourd
3. Seeds of melon
4. Seeds of cucumber

These four great seeds were bruised and rubbed in water to form an emulsion. This healing formula was used to treat catarrhal infections, bowel disorders, and urinary infections. Next time you are cleaning a member of the great seed family, you might think twice before throwing away such a precious cache of healing medicines!

Melon Trivia

> The word "pumpkin" is derived from the older name "pompion."

> English melons were once called "millions," hence the current name "melon."

> Squash *(Cucurbita melopepo, C. evifera, C. pepo)* are called "marrows" in England.

> Melons are very diverse. The largest, *Cucurbita maxima,* is a gourd; the smallest is the size of an olive. They can be globular, egg-shaped, spindle-shaped, or serpentine in shape. The skin is netted, ribbed, furrowed, or smooth. The flesh can be white, green, yellow, or orange.

> The melon fruit is eaten or juiced.

> The root of the melon can be used as a purgative.

> An active bitter substance in melon root makes an emetic.

Calabash *(Lagenaria siceraria)*

The calabash or bottle gourd is not just a container for the Orisha Osayin; it is also a useful tool. Bottle gourd has great symbolic importance to the Yoruba. A calabash is used as a float during fishing, which may explain how the gourd was able to establish itself across the Atlantic Ocean. The enslaved Jamaican people were given an extremely small allotment of personal goods during the early 1700s: a mat to lie on, an earthen pot for cooking,[3] and a calabash, which was used as a cup, bowl, spoon, and musical instrument resembling a lute. Numerous groups of transplanted African people used the small gourds as water cups and bottles and the large gourds as storage jars.[4]

ADR Path: Regla de Ocha

In the Americas and Caribbean, a path influenced by Ifa called *Regla de Ocha* (Rule of the Orisha) represents Osayin as the guiro (gourd) that hangs in the Santeria *ile* (house-temple). Tribute needs to be paid to Osayin before his herbal medicine can be used in ceremony, spells, and cures. Osayin's symbols include the gourd where his spirit resides, a twisted tree branch, and his color—green.

— SP☆TLIGHT —

Squash of Winter, Squash of Summer

I remember squash season so clearly by the celebratory attitude of my mother at its arrival. She simply loved squash; we'd typically buy them from nearby roadside fruit and vegetable stands in or near Quinton, New Jersey. Then, once home, my mother would wash them, pat them dry, and lightly sauté them with an onion in butter in a cast-iron skillet. Her favorites were the pretty little green and yellow pattypan squash that look like a crown for a small creature.

Squash are easy to grow, as long as you have space or a good pot system set up for aerial growth, and during the summer they are great  producers. The flowers can be eaten raw, fried, sautéed, or stuffed. Familiar summer squash *(Cucurbita pepo)* include pattypan (bush scallop), crookneck (summer crookneck), and zucchini.

In the olden days when enslaved Africans were working the fields, they had two meals a day—one at dawn and one at dusk. According to a survivor of enslavement, Bailey Cunningham, a typical meal consisted of cymblin (squash soup).[5]

Today we are free from enslavement and have many vegetables available year-round. The winter squash, an important food to our ancestors, brings tremendous holistic health benefits because it provides a soul connection through food.

Winter squash include butternut (*Cucurbita moschata*), acorn (*C. pepo*), hubbard (*C. maxima*), pumpkin (*C. maxima, C. moschata, C. pepo*), and spaghetti squash (*C. pepo*).[6] The spaghetti squash is an unusual squash and can actually be served in several different ways. I like it as a vegetarian entree, baked about forty-five minutes, flaked and covered in a marinara sauce with cheese. It's a gluten-free pasta substitute for those sensitive to gluten or reducing carbohydrate intake.

News Flash

Anything you can do with sweet potatoes (yams), you can do with winter squash, including making muffins, pies, and breads. Moreover, they are delicious roasted or used in hearty winter soups.

Vegetable Sponge *(Luffa cylindrical)*, aka Loofah

To be palatable, luffa has to be harvested and eaten while it is very young. A use for the mature luffa and the one you may be most familiar with is as a tool for an exfoliating scrub of the face or body. The luffa is wonderful for scrubbing the heels, elbows, or anywhere else you have dry skin. On the face, use gently to exfoliate, remove blackheads and whiteheads, and generally add a healthy glow to the face. Some types of luffa are used as dishcloths and for scrubbing pots and pans.

Luffa in the Medicine Cabinet

A sponge cucumber *(Luffa operculata)* helps with seasonal allergies. Intrigued to find a member of the luffa family lurking about in the ingredients list of my allergy medicine, I researched to find out why. According to my findings, recent evidence-based studies[7,8] suggest *Luffa operculata* reduces itching and runny noses as well as watering eyes experienced by sufferers of hay fever and similar upper respiratory disorders. It is efficient, well tolerated, and improves quality of life, with no reported side effects. It is combined with other natural ingredients and sold as a homeopathic treatment under the trade name Zicam.

Pumpkin *(Cucurbita pepo)*

The pumpkin, an herbaceous plant, is called *apakyi* in Ghana. It is utilized as a container for selling *aboloo* (steamed cassava dough) as well as storing clothing, and as a float in fishing. The pumpkin is revered in Africa since it can hold up to four gallons of water. Baby pumpkin is eaten, as well as the leafy shoots, called *krobonko,* which are served as a vegetable. The outside is used while the inside is discarded.[9] Some of the pumpkin stem is used to make buttons.[10] Fluted pumpkin *(Telfairia occidentalis)* is wildcrafted (gathered from natural setting rather than a cultivated area) in Ghana where it grows in the forests.[11]

Pumpkin is very high in beta-carotene antioxidants believed to fight off numerous health problems including heart attacks, cancer, and cataracts.[12] The flesh of pumpkin, and its relative, squash, can be boiled, mashed, fried, and used in sauces or served with rice.

Pumpkin Seed Oil: Another Pleasant Surprise

Herbalists recommend pumpkin seed oil applied topically to the face or taken by the level teaspoon twice a day as a treatment for acne.

Pumpkin Seeds

> Pumpkin seeds contain 30 percent reddish fixed oil, traces of a volatile oil, proteins, sugar, starches, and fiber. Pumpkin seeds also contain the amino acid curcurbitin, an antiparasitic.

> The seeds can be enjoyed roasted when ripe but must *not* be used if more than a month old.

> Pumpkin seed has been used medicinally, as a skin conditioner, for example, and is a part of the official German Pharmacopoeia, Tenth Edition.

> The Commission E has approved pumpkin seeds for the treatment of irritable bladder.

> Consumption of pumpkin seeds may help reduce bladder stones in children.[13]

> Pumpkin seeds are an inexpensive, nutritious snack, a good source of protein, and a great way to enjoy multiple parts of the vegetable, lessening waste.

Watermelon and the Kalahari !Kung

Domesticated in Africa around four thousand years ago, watermelons grow worldwide, especially in regions with long, dry, hot summers. The wild *Cucurbita lanatus* grows in Africa. In Southern Africa, it grows in the Kalahari where it is called *tasamma*. The hunter-gatherer people of the Kalahari, called the !Kung, have always had a tough life, and things are only getting more politically and economically challenging for them in the twenty-first century. Today they battle introduced diseases and struggle against all odds to retain their lifestyle. As one of few remaining hunter-gatherer groups in Africa, they experience prejudice and mistreatment from all Africans, regardless of color or ethnicity.

The !Kung people live in different camps in the Dobe area of the northwestern Kalahari. One of the fascinating aspects of these people is that, despite their hardships, they have woven healing harmoniously into the daily fabric of their lives. There is no division between sacred and mundane activities. Spiritual life is an inextricable part of their lifestyle. Every night is healing time and this often involves trance and ecstatic dancing. The !Kung do not have separate categories for the sacred, ordinary, profane, art, herbalism, or religion—all is life enjoyed in a holistic manner. All come together into a rich stew that is their culture. Their deities are as flawed as humans, and, up in the sky, they contemplate their own betrayals, sexual antics, and needs.

The people spend twelve to nineteen hours per week hunting and gathering food. There is much more gathering than hunting and the gathering is women's work; 60 to 80 percent of their food is wild-crafted vegetables. They eat the protein-rich mongongo nut, which is a major staple for the !Kung. They also dig various roots from the ground with a digging stick that is handmade, and of course they eat the juicy Kalahari melon.

The heat of the desert and monsoonal rain calls for sharing. There can be no hoarding of resources; if that were to happen, the food would quickly rot. Moreover, !Kung society is based on interdependence. If each group did not look out for all members, then they would quickly be wiped out by the elements. The !Kung relish the chance to share; they do it forthrightly, intentionally, and with great care. Sharing is the cornerstone of their society.

Num

By our standards, the !Kung of the Kalahari are a deeply spiritual people. They call spiritual energy *num,* and it is something to be cultivated on a daily basis. Num is raised through dancing. The healers held in the highest regard are called *ama ama* and they are revered. Prayers to deities can take place anytime and anywhere. The !Kung speak plainly to the goddess and the gods; the great god is Goo Na and the lesser one is Kautha. These deities live in the sky. Typical prayers are:

• Give us your water (meaning rain)

• Let food grow

• Give us a chance to rest

Different groups gather around the water holes so that they have water when it is available. When it is not, they have the good fortune of having the watery melon that grows wild in their desert. The Kalahari melon looks much like a melon we might purchase from the watermelon man's truck or a local farmer's market—deep green rind, soft red flesh, and dark seeds. The melon is an important source of nutrition and replenishment for the indigenous people and for those who travel through the Kalahari.[14]

Pass the Seeds, Please

Whereas in the United States we have made an art of spitting out the seeds, and folklore stories abound about what dreadful thing might happen if we happen to swallow the seeds, the Kalahari !Kung eat the seeds. If you think about it, this is not a farfetched idea. After all, we consume the seeds of watermelon's kin—pumpkin, cucumber, and squash.

Traditionally, the Kalahari seeds are extracted from the fruit and roasted over a fire, then ground fine. The pulverized seed is high in protein and good eating. The hunting-gathering people of the Kalahari chew it first and then moisten it with saliva to use

Kalahari Seed Oil

Kalahari seed oil products are making their way into the Australian, North American, and European Union botanical beauty markets. A number of promising product lines have cropped up featuring the Kalahari melon seed, including the oil used for massages, face treatments, and general skin care, and the gel used to revitalize puffy, tired eyes.

the seed powder cosmetically. This paste is spread across the body, bringing a smooth, healthy, rose-tinged gloss to their medium-brown skin color. There is also a bitter form of the wild melon used medicinally, even though it would be poisonous if used by the unskilled.[15]

Watermelon Elsewhere in Africa

The *Citrullus colocynthis* watermelon is cultivated in the southern savanna and in North Africa. The *Citrullus lanatus* watermelon is native to Central Africa where it is a vital source of water. Watermelons are almost always available in urban markets in season. There is an incredible variety in melons in terms of shape and sizes available; some varieties are grown just for the seeds. Melons are a staple food that is refreshing to both human and animals in North Africa and parts of the Middle East. It is a native of tropical Africa and the East Indies. Lake Burullus, east of the Rosetta channel of the Nile, is particularly noted for their watermelon, which is yellow inside. There are numerous crops in the Northern Hemisphere from May until November. The food value of the seeds is 45 percent fat and 54 percent protein. The seeds are also used as a passable coffee substitute.

Watermelon has high amounts of lycopene and glutathione, antioxidant and anticancer compounds. The gorgeous pink fruit is mildly antibacterial, antiviral, and shows promise as an anticoagulant.[17] In Africa, *egusi* is made from ground melon seeds and used to thicken stews. In the United States, watermelon is the most consumed melon on the market, and forty-four states produce more than fifty varieties of this thirst-quenching treat.

Plucky Glutathione

Many of the healing soul foods explored in this chapter (including okra and squash) contain high amounts of glutathione per recommended serving, but you may wonder what it is. Glutathione helps block cell damage from toxic compounds such as environmental pollutants (indoors and out) and helps detoxify the body. Glutathione appears to deactivate at least thirty cancer-causing substances.[16]

Honeydew and Cantaloupe

True cantaloupe is *Cucumis cantalupensis;* what we refer to as cantaloupe is actually a muskmelon *(Cucumis melo),* as true cantaloupes only grow in a small part of Italy. 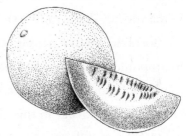 One variety of the muskmelon is the honeydew. Muskmelon is an annual trailing herb with large palmate lobed leaves, tendrils, and deep, bell-shaped corolla on the flowers.

> Muskmelon has blood-thinning capacity.
> Melon root is used as a purgative and emetic in some traditional medicine.
> Orange-fleshed melons contain ample antioxidants.[18]
> Green honeydew is a useful way of replenishing moisture in the body and it quenches the thirst during the heat of summer.
> One new area of investigation is the antiplatelet aggregation and anticoagulant (deterring blood clots) qualities of melon.

Cucumber *(Cucumis sativus)*

Cucumbers are wonderful raw, in salad, juiced alone or with other vegetables, or in cold soup. They seem to have a cooling effect and are recommended for summer and as an accompaniment to hot foods, such as curries, in a dish called *raita,* which also contains yogurt.

Cucumber is used cosmetically in facial masks, particularly to help revive tired eyes. Placing two cooled cucumber slices over the eyes encourages rest and replenishment at home and at day spas. They purportedly reduce dark circles around the eyes and help with puffiness. The cold  temperature of chilled cucumber would alone help reduce puffiness in the way ice does, yet the smooth texture of the vegetable is more comfortable. Many people enjoy the thinner-skinned, seedless, hydroponically grown cucumber, also called English cucumber, though it is now grown in many locations. The seeds also have benefits, as noted earlier in this chapter. Cucumbers also contain antioxidants especially good at fighting skin cancer.[19]

Enslaved Africans brought this little cousin to the cucumber to the New World. Gherkin is believed to be a cultivated and altered form of the African species of *Cucumis prophetarium* or *C. figarei,* even though they are both perennial and the Caribbean species is annual. It is a much sought-after food,  eaten raw, cooked, and especially pickled. Gherkins accompany meals and are a snack food. In pickled gherkins, the "juice," which is primarily vinegar, is used in preparation of cold salads and is consumed as a healthy drink.

Melon: Juicy Fruit for the Soul

Not long ago, middle-class blacks, and those aspiring to be, shunned melon. This was in large part due to the days of the minstrel show, when products, advertisers, and actors denigrated African culture using the foods we brought with us to the New World, such as melons. African Americans depicted as low-class, "country" people, also called pickaninnies, were shown eating watermelon, spitting the seeds through gaps between their teeth.

Today, it is important to realize that eating melons, in their myriad forms, offers a way to stay connected with the unique aspect of our culture while also gaining enormous health benefits. Melons, one of the juiciest of fruits, are healing in a holistic way as they bring culture and nutrition together. No wonder they remain a central feature in our summer gatherings, reunions, and other celebrations.

Osayin's Green Bounty

While the family Cucurbitaceae brings Osayin's calabash immediately to mind, there are a few other precious gifts that are related to him as well. These soul foods include greens. Green is Osayin's color and it also represents the verdant essence of Mother Earth. Osayin's array of greens represents fertility, vitality, and health. Greens also instill these traits in us, building our resistance to illness and strengthening our entire system.

Whereas once people thought greens, such as collard, mustard, and turnip (tops), were a lowly food, now people all around the world celebrate the nutrient-rich gift of Osayin's greens. You can also find them in upscale groceries catering to the organic crowd, like Whole Foods Market.

Greens in the Diaspora

> In West Africa, the preferred green is called bitterleaf, which is washed to remove its bitter taste.
> Cassava leaves are enjoyed, as are *ewedu,* red sorrel, *yakuwa, lansun,* and pumpkin leaves.
> Jamaica has made callaloo[20] a much loved vegetable, and seafood stew featuring their unique greens is variously called dasheen, Chinese spinach, taro tops, or callaloo bush.
> In Africa and the diaspora, beet tops, kale, and spinach are some of the greens enjoyed.

Greens, Lutein, and the Eyes

Greens are especially high in lutein, chlorophyll, and antioxidants. Lutein is the main antioxidant that helps the eyes. Of all the green vegetables, kale is number one, collard greens are number two, and spinach is number three in terms of concentration of lutein.[21] Greens are showing promise as a deterrent for macular degeneration. This ailment consists of a deterioration of the sensitive central region of the retina, which weakens the field of vision.

Collard, mustard, and turnip greens need not be overcooked or super-fatted to be tasty, which is what we've done historically. The soul food we enjoy is packed with antioxidant vitamins and minerals—especially wholesome when not overwhelmed by animal fat. In Asian cuisine, such as Thai food, collards and other greens are stir-fried and they are *delicious,* showing there is no need to cook the greens so long they turn dull and lifeless.

Just a Thought

Try your leafy vegetables such as collard, mustard, and turnip greens seasoned with apple cider vinegar and sautéed in olive or palm oil with onion and cayenne. If you want to cook them more in accordance with tradition, which amounts to stewed greens, by all means drink the broth (pot liquor) for additional health benefits.

Or try braising greens in light olive oil, a dash of salt, apple cider, or balsamic vinegar, seasoned with cayenne and garlic, then simmering them in chicken broth for about 20 minutes to retain their goodness.

Seasoned Cast Iron

Traditionally, our people have enjoyed cooking these greens in a cast-iron Dutch oven. Cooking greens in cast iron and adding a dash of vinegar or splash of lemon makes them even richer in iron than they normally are. Some folks cook greens with tomato, which interacts with the cast iron in the same way as vinegar or lemon, enhancing their iron-rich quality. Because they are high in calcium, greens are an excellent food for young people who are having growth spurts as well as pregnant women and the elderly. To keep the pan "seasoned," do not let it rust by soaking it in water like normal skillets. Wipe with a soapy-water sponge and rinse with a clear-water sponge. Towel dry. Pour some vegetable oil onto a paper towel. Rub this around the skillet, covering all surfaces; this is called "seasoning the skillet" and it retains flavors while deterring rust.

Clean and Green

One of the reasons people often reserve greens (be they collard, mustard, turnip, or even spinach and kale) for special occasions is the challenge of cleaning them. I remember my grandmother and mother soaking them overnight in the bathtub, and following in their footsteps, I have done this, too. Soaking your greens in the sink and adding vinegar to the water accelerates the cleaning process; no more overnight soaking. For those craving convenience, many stores now carry pre-cleaned and chopped greens and spinach.

— SP✷TLIGHT—

Okra

Another of Osayin's green wonders is okra (*Abelmoschus esculentus L. Moench*), also called *guiabo, guimgombo, ochroes, gumbo,* and *ocro.* It was introduced to the Americas from Africa. A synonym for okra on both sides of the Atlantic is gumbo; even though it is spelled differently in West Africa than it is in the diaspora, the meaning is the same. In *Africanism in the Gullah Dialect,*[22] Lorenzo Turner identified words from various African languages in Gullah patois, for example, *gombo,* "okra," from the Tsiluba and Umbundu languages.

This complex, vitamin-rich vegetable changes the quality of our beloved stew that also bears its name—gumbo!

Okra has pointed ridged green pods with a stem at one end. There are ample white seeds inside. The more they are chopped, the more thickening agent is released. Okra is best picked young because that is when the pods are less fibrous and more tender. The pod is eaten boiled and used as a stew thickener;[23] the leaves are used for their softening ability cosmetically, medicinally, and as a nourishing whole food. Okra is very high in the antioxidant alpha-lipoic acid.[24]

Another okra *(Hibiscus esculentus),* cultivated in the Sudan, Guinea, and savanna woodland countries of West Africa and used as a backyard crop, is eaten in soup or stews, sliced, dried, and stored. It is high in calcium and relieves constipation.[25]

Okra of either species, like the Curcubitaceae family's squash, is rich in the antioxidant glutathione, among other healthy constituents.

Some early uses of okra in the Gullah community include:

• Eating the blossoms and pod as well as the seeds.
• Sautéing the blossoms in the same way as squash blossoms.
• Roasting the seeds as a coffee substitute.

Okra blossoms are used in two types of poultice:

• Applied to sores that won't heal.
• Mixed with soap and sugar and applied to wounds to speed healing.[26]

Black-Eyed Pea *(Vigna unguiculata)*

One of my favorites, these "peas," also called cowpeas, are actually tasty legumes. In West Africa, a snack made of black-eyed peas is called *kosai* and *moyin-moyin*. My love of these legumes is not far-flung; black-eyed peas were so beloved by the enslaved Africans that they brought them with them to the New World. The peas are nutritious, inexpensive, easy to grow, and easy to cook; they are sustaining and nurturing to our soul (that is why they are called soul food). A large study showed that those who eat beans every week are 40 percent less likely to die of pancreatic cancer.[27] This is because of the protease inhibitors in legumes.

Black-eyed peas are lucky charms, as are many other types of legumes around the world. Black-eyed peas are a featured food at our New Year's meal, and in that way they have become a part of our black cultural celebration of Kwanzaa (the last day, New Year's, includes a feast).

> Black-eyed peas are thought to usher in silver money and are served with white rice, which symbolizes fertility and longevity, as well as stewed tomato, which is symbolic of love and sensuality.

> Corn bread accompanies the meal and brings with it additional blessings from the Corn Mothers.

> As soul food, black-eyed peas were traditionally cooked with pork, though this is changing for health reasons. Today, many people either cook them as a vegetarian meal or replace the pork with smoked turkey wings or drumsticks, or chicken.

Honey: Sweetness of the Goddess and the God

One of the most endearing images of honey in recent memory was the unifying element in the novel *The Secret Life of Bees,* by Sue Monk Kidd. In this tale set in South Carolina, three sisters named May, June, and August take in a white girl named Lily and her housekeeper Rosaleen. Gradually, they allow the two newcomers into their spiritual world, which includes synchronized rituals with a circle of women, celebrating the Black Madonna and freedom from slavery using honey. They ceremoniously pour honey over the head of the Black Madonna who is chained. As the honey drizzles down the statue's body, the chains loosen. The Black Madonna, like the black people, enjoys the sweetness of freedom.[28]

In an older, nonfiction account, anthropologist Colin Turnbull describes even more intriguing accounts of black folk interacting magically with honey. He shares observations of the honey dance and honey ritual of the Forest People, who are small in stature and reside in the Ituri Forest of the Congo. Turnbull reported that there were special games during honey harvest season. Men would pretend to be honey gatherers, dancing in a long, sensual, curvilinear line. They would look up exaggeratedly as if searching for bees. The women were the honeybees. They would appear, singing in a soft rhythmic buzz, buzz, and buzz chant. The women would tap the men on the head and sparks would literally fly (this was a love and harvest ritual). There was a fire at the hearth of special woods for the occasion and indigenous leaves moistened so they would smoke rather than flame. The combination of flame and smoke billowed upward. Men would blow their honey whistles, while women clapped their hands and sang, hoping the calls would travel with the smoke, calling the bees to make more honey.[29]

Honey use weaves through ancient Egyptian apothecaries, recipes, and ritual devotion. It was an important ingredient in kyphi, a unique Egyptian incense used to pay homage to the God Ra and Goddess Isis, which also contains dried fruit, red wine, and resins. Honey was used to mix a kohl solution to paint the eyes. It was also used cosmetically in hair and facial care.

Honey across Africa

West Africa: In Mali, *soume* is an alcoholic drink derived from honey. Soume is consumed from a calabash. Around the calabash and under the influence of soume, young people learn the secrets of their community. The elders gather around the soume-filled calabash to brag, remember, and gossip.[30]

East Africa: The Samburu people mix milk from their cattle with honey and pour it as a libation for spiritual blessing of the land. They use blood from the cattle and honey as a libation in a land-cleansing rite. They have done this publicly in recent times as a gesture of peace with neighbors with whom there have been land disputes.

Southern Africa: The Bemba people of Zambia in Southern Africa enjoy all of the healing foods in this chapter along with grain and honey as an important part of their sustenance.

Honey in the Sacred Life of the Diaspora

Caribbean and the Americas: In the Black Atlantic, the honey Orisha is Oshun; in Brazil, Oxun; and in Cuba, Ochun. Oshun is invoked to bring healthy children, easy childbirth, love, sensuality, beauty, refinement, and sweetness. The people of Trinidad and Tobago Islands demonstrate how honey of Oshun is used in blessing, ritual, and ceremony.

> They prepare it with water, brandy, olive oil, and sugar and place it in a calabash as an offering to Oshun during some thanksgiving rites.

> Devotees consume an offering that includes duck, honey, olive oil, sugar, and brandy.

> A libation of honey, lavender, brandy, and olive oil is poured in honor of Oshun, also called Goddess of Water Powers and sometimes referred to as Saint Philomene.

> A honey dressing is rubbed on a bamboo pole to invoke the spirit of Oshun.

> A table is laid with honey, a calabash, candles, grains, and flowers to honor Oshun.

Jewels of the Golden Hive

Although it might not have immediately leapt into your head as a soul food per se, honey and our friends the bees are very important to African cultures and within the broader diaspora for both mundane and sacred activities. Our friends the bees produce many other items of great use to the herbalist. In addition to honey, we are accustomed to:

Beeswax: Used to thicken creams, salves, balms, pomades, and soap. Beeswax is also used on magickal seals and practical seals to firmly close corked bottles of elixir, potion, or brews.

Propolis: Used by bees to seal the hive, this bee medicine protects them from bacteria, viruses, and fungi and is used by people for the same reason.

Honey:[31] Can be derived from various flowers and herbs; medicinal content varies with the flower that is its source (medicinal qualities follow).

Raw honey: This is straight from the beehive; it may be strained, but no heating is involved.

Commercial raw honey: This type of honey has a minimal amount of processing.

Royal jelly: As its name suggests, royal jelly is fed to the young larva that eventually grows up to become Queen Bee. Royal jelly contains an antibacterial protein called royalisin. Royalisin is rich in amino acids and is an effective deterrent for staph and strep species of bacteria.[32] Royal jelly shows potential as an antitumor substance. In the Japanese research, royal jelly had a significant effect on treating sarcoma cells but no effect on leukemia cells in a lab test.[33]

Whipped honey: The naturally occurring glucose spontaneously crystallizes and the crystallization is controlled, yielding a creamy honey. This is a dense, rich honey product that can be spread on toast like peanut butter.

Honey is a part of story, song, dance, ritual, and economic opportunity for Africans and people of African descent. It is also a tasty way to sweeten teas and baked goods, allowing us to cut down on sugar consumption. Honey is sensual and it is useful in lovemaking rites as an edible body balm. It is also an excellent cosmetic, making an easy facial that controls oily skin, a soothing instant lip balm, and a softening hair conditioner—go easy and rinse well!

Medicinal Applications of Honey

Topical:

> Apply to cracked lips as healing balm.
> Apply to cuts as antimicrobial, antiseptic.
> Apply directly to eyelids for inflammation and conjunctivitis.
> Apply directly to foot ulcers (diabetic) and cover with a dressing and secondary dressing to keep honey from seeping.
> Apply directly to burns.
> Apply to wounds to speed healing and as a slight antiseptic.

Oral:

> Add to tea or drinks by the level teaspoon for an energy boost.
> Take by the teaspoon with lemon as a sore throat soother for colds and coughs.
> Take when you have a hangover; honey aids in the liver's oxidation (breakdown process) of alcohol.
> Heart benefits are suggested from tests that indicate increased antioxidants in the blood after consumption of honey, which helps to lower cholesterol and keep arteries from hardening. Apply to meat to soften texture while cooking (marinade) and to fight food-borne pathogens. It is thought that honey traps free radicals from meat as it cooks.

> Take honey to reduce stress and anxiety. It is considered a mild tranquilizer and is a preferred additive to relaxing herbal teas like chamomile, catnip, and skullcap for that reason.

Other:

> Used diluted with distilled water as a douche for vaginal yeast infection.

Constituents

> Phytochemicals
> Antioxidants: flavonoids, ascorbic acid, alkaloids
> Antimicrobial substances, including the enzyme glucose oxidase
> Boron: Boron is an especially important constituent of honey. Boron increases blood levels of estrogen and other compounds that prevent calcium loss and consequential bone demineralization. Boron increases steroids in the blood.

Onward

Having considered what is above, it is time to see what is below—roots and tubers. We close this chapter and Osayin's calabash for now, sealed with honey, the natural product that is a supreme mind, body, and spirit healer.

CHAPTER 6

SO IT IS BELOW: ROOTING FOR GOOD HEALTH

"R oot" is an important word in African American culture. We celebrate our roots—just as they are the foundation from which plants grow, so they are the source of our rich culture. The notion of roots has transformed over time and adapted to different spaces: In Africa, people are rooted to their people, clan or secret society, village and spiritual practice; in the Caribbean and Americas, people have roots that tie them to a specific island, a part of the country, one coast or another, neighborhoods, or in some cases specific counties. Still reeling from our uprooting from Africa, it has become something of a cultural passion for us to try to find our roots in the Motherland and other cultures using genealogy and DNA genealogy. Meanwhile, a unifying element that holds us together culturally is our food, herbs, and specific ways of naming as well as preparing them. In the naming and preparation of herbs and whole foods lie important keys to our unified cultural roots as a people.

Whereas once we were isolated from one another, dispersed on different islands and scattered across huge expanses of land in the Americas and Caribbean, today we are increasingly celebrating what we have in common. We see the commonalities within African culture, whether the location is north, south, east,

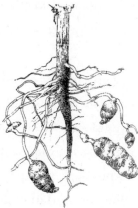

or west—not just in Africa but also in the Black Atlantic. Though we have many different branches, languages, and appearances, there is that one strong root to our tree of life that unites us as a people: Africa.

A Few Botanical Definitions

Root is the underground organ—lacking buds, leaves, or nodes—that anchors the plant in the ground. Tubers and rhizomes are often called roots, though the true root vegetables are carrots, horseradish, radishes, salsify, rutabagas, parsnips, and turnips.

Tuber is a fleshy underground bulb-like stem that serves as the reproductive food storage area of the plant and features minute leaves with buds. Examples of tubers are potatoes, sweet potatoes, yams, cassava, and Jerusalem artichoke.

Rhizome is a horizontal subterranean plant stem above the root that produces shoots above and roots below, and differs from a true root in that it features buds, nodes, and often leaves. Examples of rhizome plants are ginger, galangal, and turmeric.

This chapter investigates the healing uses of a few of our most celebrated roots, heralded for their multiple ways of making our lives more comfortable. Keep in mind that traditional African healing seeks to examine the core or root cause of a problem, which may be physical, metaphysical, environmental, or of the spirit realm. Whether used in amulets, charms, brews, potions, or tasty dishes, roots are deeply embedded in African American healing practices. Indeed, "root" connotes many different parts of our culture: symbolically, as geographical place and cultural identity; and literally, as tubers and rhizomes.

Getting to Know Your Johns: High John, Little John, and Low John

There is a character that makes multiple appearances in African American folklore—his name is John. John is referred to as Big John, John Henry, High John, High John the Conqueror, Little John, and Low John. Sometimes John is the metaphor for a formidable man with superhuman strength and integrity, as in the story of John Henry, the black folk hero and steel-driving railroad-creating man. In African American folklore, John can also be naughty or unpredictable, especially when connected to the story of the Eshu tricksters. In one story retold by Virginia Hamilton, "The Story of the Two Johns" one of the Johns is called the devil and performs brutal acts on animals, while the other John is the voice of reason. In other places in African American folklore, John becomes the symbol of courage and resilience, as in the stories of High John the Conqueror, the enslaved African who could not be bound by his chains. Here, John is the spirit of survival—a spirit that enables humans to survive disasters, atrocities, infractions, abuse, neglect, and diseases like cancer or heart disorders. High John is ultimately a radiant spirit of resilience that is at the root of all people.

High John the Conqueror *(Ipomoea jalapa)*

High John the Conqueror is a member of the morning glory family, related to our much-loved soul food, the sweet potato. High John the Conqueror is a natural amulet, and as such is put inside a charm bag called a mojo bag. High John resembles a nut and indeed may be a symbolic stand-in for testicles (we all know the metaphors that "balls" represent; chief among them is the suggestion of courage). John represents the type of spiritual energy we want to keep close to our persons, whether this sultry-smelling tuber is soaked in whiskey, dusted in magnetic sand for attraction, drenched in lucky oil like Van Van oil, or just left as is to watch over us from a night table as we sleep. This natural amulet that contains mild mind-altering constituents plays an essential role in African American spiritual magick as one of the strongest roots or tubers found in a mojo bag.

Little John Chew, Li'l Chew *(Alpinia galanga)*

Little John Chew is a member of the ginger family. Most people call Little John "galangal." The rhizome of the plant offers up a spice that tastes like a mild form of its cousin, ginger, discussed later in this chapter. You can find the powder in spice shops and specialty stores, sold most often as galangal. Like ginger, Little John Chew is perfectly safe to consume. As an herb for the body, it is a stomachic carminative that soothes bellyache and relieves gas. It has found its way into our rootwork and magickal herbalism as well.

Little John is chewed and either spit or swallowed when doing court magick or spells outside a courtroom, hence its nickname "Little John Chew." A correlation to consider: In traditional Central African and West African sculptures, spittle alone or combined with herbs is added to powerful figurative sculptures to further imbue them with that formidable energy known as *ashe*. Chewing the herb allows it to absorb the ashe and àṣẹ of the practitioner, creating an unusually powerful herb capable of doing the rootworker's bidding.

— SP✷TLIGHT —

Low John *(Trillium erectum, T. pendulum)*

A third John, Low John is a relative of the lily *(Trillium grandiflorum).* Low John is also called Beth root. The Yoruba people believe that there is great power in the naming of things. Àṣẹ power stems from understanding the name and the particular healing language of the plant when used for holistic health. High John the Conqueror, Little John Chew, and Low John were so named by people of African descent with that particular thought and distinctive way of utilizing herbs in mind.

The Johns are important tools of the rootworker, whether used to help, protect, defend, attract, strengthen, or draw luck. High John and Little John are used primarily in magickal herbalism, while Low John is used medicinally.

Are Country Roots Bad?

By convincing ourselves that we are an urban people, looking down on all things rural as "country," we have lost an important part of our heritage. In our African spiritual roots, roots like High John the Conqueror and Little John Chew have been utilized in magick and ritual. We would not consider a holiday joyous without consuming our favorite roots—sweet potatoes or yams. The mind-body-spirit schism was a malignant seed planted by others; without being nourished by us, however, such a schism could not have survived. In any case, it has yielded great harm. Rather than casually accept the separation of mind, body, and spirit that has occurred in modern history, we'd do well to weed out this pernicious belief for the sake of our spiritual enlightenment, which takes us well beyond mere survival. When we harvest roots and tubers, inevitably we touch the earth, whether we dig up the root or tuber ourselves or handle it still covered with bits of Mother Earth. This helps us heal the mind-body-spirit disconnection. Hold onto your soul foods including yams and other root vegetables, collards, and watermelon—there is great magic, mystery, cultural connection, and potential for healing stored in them.

The Ubiquitous Yam

The word "yam" is derived from the Guinea word *nyami,* meaning something to eat because it is an important food. Portuguese slave traders could not pronounce *nyami.* It was called *igname* in French and, of course, "yam" in English. The family name of yams is Dioscoreaceae, named for the Greek botanist thought to be the first physician in Europe. These starchy tubers can weigh as much as thirty pounds each and are food for humans as well as animal fodder. The words "yam" and "sweet potato" are often used interchangeably to describe a beloved African tuber, but the conflation is not botanically correct. Sweet potatoes are in a different family. Both of these tubers, however, are an important part of African diets; they come from the earth, and are celebrated in connection to culture and spirit.

African Yam

True yams grow in Africa and the Caribbean. If you find African yams sold in the United States, they are usually sold in Latino neighborhood shops under the name *Africanoes.* There are a variety of African yams, including:

Cush-cush yam *(Dioscorea trifida):* Grown primarily in the Caribbean, it is one of the four most important food yams in the world. Surprisingly enough, when cooking, it smells a lot like bacon

━━

How to Give Thanksgiving to the Earth Mother, Ela

When you are preparing your yam/sweet potatoes during special observances, put one on a mantel, windowsill, or altar and invoke the Earth Goddess by chanting softly, *"Pa isu Ela . . . Pa isu Ela . . . Pa isu Ela,"* continuing as long as you like. In the manner of a mantra, it will provide some relaxation during hectic times. It also is a gesture of thanksgiving to the earth.

and eggs. The compact, ivory-fleshed tuber has a rosy under-layer beneath its skin. The tubers turn dry and fluffy when cooked and taste like a fluffy, smoked potato.

White Guinea yam *(D. rotunda):* Originally from West Africa, this yam is used to make the popular dish called *fufu* (a thick paste or porridge). It stores well and is tolerant of a long, dry season. White Guinea yam might be a useful plant to grow in the United States because it does not require a lot of water, a resource we have a tendency to overuse.

Transatlantic Yam Festivals

The Igbo people of Nigeria believe in an almighty god named ChuKu (Chineke). The affiliated gods are Ela, the Earth Mother; Anyanu, the sun; and Iwa, the sky. Ela is connected to the Egun (the ancestors). Ndiche and Ajoku are associated with yams. The ancestors come to the annual festivals as marked dancers called *Mmno,* becoming a part of the community.

The Igala, another group residing in Nigeria, have a central society formed around the Egun, which are remembered, honored, and venerated during yam harvest. A portion of yam from the harvest must go to Ela, the Earth Mother, as an offering to her before it is eaten. This is called *Pa isu Ela*. Orisha Orunmila also partakes in the ceremonial offering of the yam. No wonder sweet potatoes, used interchangeably with yams in the United States, are so important to our annual harvest celebration of Thanksgiving.

Ike Ji Aro is another festival in Nigeria. It is a celebration of the new yam among the Aro people. This festival, also called *Ahiajoku*, takes place each year between August and October. It is popular among farming communities.

Yambilee in Louisiana

The sweet potato *(Ipomoea batatas)*, called yam, is a very important crop for the region of southwest Louisiana. Each year the yam is thanked for its goodness in a festival called Yambilee. The people in this area also cut roots, rhizomes, and tubers ritualistically to serve as natural amulets placed in the mojo bag. This practice echoes the birthing ritual that follows.

Deity: Orisha Orunmila

Orunmila is the lawgiver of the Orishas and voice of Olorun (the first Orisha, born of Mawu, mother of the gods) in the land of Ife. Olorun carries an ever-burning torch.

Yam Birthing Ritual: Isu Egbegbe

True yams contain diosgenin, which acts as a precursor to the female hormone, estrogen. The African yam birthing ritual is a part of the African practice of *agbo adoyun,* which translates as "liquefied herbs for pregnant women." I found this ritual to be of great interest because it unites the medicinal qualities of yam (its herbal uses for women) with its earth symbolism.

*WARNING: I am only sharing this as a story so that you understand the depth of importance of yam in African societies; this is not something you should do on your own without an ATR leader to guide you (especially if you are pregnant). The consequences could be deadly.

African farmers noticed the yam is near the top of the soil in the morning and is located lower in the earth as dusk approaches. This change in position is seen as mimicking the course of a woman's pregnancy; the child is higher in the womb earlier in the pregnancy, dropping lower later, and eventually traversing the birth canal during birth. *Isu Egbegbe* ("the Mysterious Yam") is a ritual that honors this symbolism.

Here is how the ritual goes:

1. Healers put a yam cut into pieces into a bottle.
2. The bottle is filled with water.
3. A hole, signifying the vagina, is pierced in the cover, which in turn suggests the round cervix.
4. A feather of a beautiful bird is placed inside the hole (mucous plug).
5. The bottle is hung; it cannot touch the ground (reflecting the sacred view of the pregnant woman).
6. The yam-infused water is consumed, half a cup at a time once every three days. This causes vomiting, which is considered normal and may act out a desired course of action: the body's rejection of illness, toxins, and disease.[1]

This practice is believed to prevent convulsions in the newborn. Again, because of the purgative quality of this ritual, it should only be done with the supervision of a traditional African medicine person.

— SP✳TLIGHT —

Wild Yam *(Dioscorea villosa)*

Wild yam is related to the African yam but not to what we call a sweet potato or yam in the United States. Wild yam is a perennial climbing vine, native to eastern North America and New England; it is found in the north from Minnesota to Ontario and in the south from Florida to Texas. Wild yam grows well in damp woods, swamps, thickets, roadside fences, and hedges, and it prefers a sandy to loamy medium well-drained, moist soil in partial shade. The prominently veined leaves rest on trailing vines.

Wild yam is edible and medicinal. Ailments treated by ancient healers include a plethora of female reproductive organ complaints, including managing PMS and painful or absent periods, childbirth pains, and menopause. The wild yam contains high concentrations of dioscin, which is converted chemically into diosgenin, used to manufacture progesterone and other steroid drugs to treat reproductive organs and ailments such as asthma and arthritis. Diosgenin enabled the creation of the contraceptive pill. Research at Brigham Young University demonstrates that curing the yam (letting it dry and age) increases the concentration of diosgenin.

Other constituents of wild yam—phytosterols[2] (beta-sitosterol), alkaloids, and tannins—make it a powerful anti-inflammatory, antispasmodic, cholagogue, diaphoretic, diuretic, peripheral vasodilator, and relaxant.

Part used: rhizome.

Usage: tincture (solution of herb preserved in alcohol or glycerin), capsules, or tea. To make tea, decoct 8 ounces of water and 1 ounce of dried, cut, and sifted root for 25 minutes; drink half a cup twice daily.

Constituents: phytosterols, alkaloids, tannins, steroidal saponins, and dioscin (which yields diosgenin).

With all of its seemingly miraculous qualities, it is easy to understand how wild yam has become overused in our society. United Plant Savers[3] has listed wild yam as an endangered plant. Care should be taken to seek substitutes and to preserve the plant by growing it yourself rather than buying it in volume or wildcrafting it.[4]

Medicine for the Triple Goddess Aspect of Women

As you can see, this plant is suitable for the Triple Goddess aspects (Maiden, Mother, Crone archetype) and the various stages in between experienced during womanhood. Wild yam is used to relieve hot flashes, night sweats, mood changes, and vaginal dryness experienced by the crone. It has applications for males and females of all ages as well. Wild yam is used to treat irritable bowel syndrome (IBS), gastritis, gallbladder ailments, and spasmodic cramps. In small doses, it may help the nausea experienced by pregnant women. Additionally, the diuretic quality soothes the urinary tract, and works well with any imbalances in the body including the root causes of irritability.

As a relaxant, it curbs stress and tension and shows promise at quelling the threat of miscarriage. As a food, wild yam contains twice the amount of potassium as bananas, one of our higher potassium foods.

Sweet Potato *(Ipomoea batatas)*

Beloved as a soul food in the African American community, eaten as a starchy vegetable boiled or roasted, this tuberous root has many phytonutrients and constituents that lend it its reputation as a health and soul food.

Suggested amount: half a cup daily

Preparation: roasted, boiled, baked, mashed—easy on butter and salt.

Here are some highlights that make sweet potato a valuable contributor to wellness:

1. The sweet potato has a laxative effect due to its high fiber content, and it can be used medicinally to regulate bowels and to encourage a good complexion.

2. Sweet potatoes have some of the most disease-fighting antioxidants of all vegetables.

3. Eating half a cup of beta-carotene-rich[5] sweet potato every day dramatically reduces the chances of heart attack or stroke in women, according to a Harvard University Study that tracked ninety thousand women over an eight-year period.

4. Sweet potatoes' high beta-carotene content makes them apt at helping the body boost its natural immunity, which reduces the chances of cancer, even if only a small amount is consumed every day. This suggestion carries over to lung cancer, one of the most deadly forms of cancer, for smokers

or nonsmokers, and even applies to those already diagnosed with cancer.

5. Sweet potatoes help fight viral and bacterial infections.[6]

6. Sweet potatoes help deter cataract growth.

In short, sweet potatoes, that kindly comfort food we eat each Thanksgiving, Christmas, New Year's, and on other holy days, is a powerhouse root to tap into for good health. For a more wholesome experience, reach for roasted sweet potatoes rather than candied sweet potatoes.

Cassava

Cassava is also called maioc, mandioca, yucca, sagu, and tapioca and is second only to sweet potato in terms of importance as an African staple food and economic crop. Native to Central or South America, it is the only member of the spurge family of plants to supply food. Cassava will grow where other things will not, and, because of that, it is very valuable in areas without fertile soil or good growing conditions. Cassava has been cultivated since 2500 BCE. Today, Brazil and Indonesia are top producers of cassava. Cassava is a low-protein, high-starch (energy) food.

Yucca and Cacabi

The word "yucca," pronounced yoo-ka, comes from the Arawak (indigenous) people of the Orinoco Basin who settled Greater and Lesser Antilles. The Portuguese took the crop to West Africa and it spread elsewhere from there. "Yucca" refers to the roots, whereas "cacabi" refers to the bread made from them.

Bitter cassava *(Manihot esculenta)* is distinguished from sweet cassava *(Manihot palmata)*. The liquid of bitter cassava was used in earlier times, recorded in the daily activities of the enslaved Africans in the New World. The poisonous juices were used to cast worms out of meat and out of humans. Expelling worms is a particularly important physical aspect of West African healing, and this concern was brought to the New World, especially as we doctored ourselves.

Cassava is prepared as food in many different ways around the world. The types of cassava grown in Africa and Brazil contain cyanide, which must be extracted before the cassava can be consumed. The types imported in the United States come from Costa Rica and the Dominican Republic and do not contain cyanide.

> Flour called *farinha* is made in Brazil.

> The flour called *gari* in Africa is used to make flat breads.

> Cassava is eaten mashed or boiled as a vegetable or as dumplings and cakes, and it is even mixed with coconut and sweetener to make biscuits.

> The West Indian dish pepper pot features cassava.

> Africa produces eighty-two million tons of cassava annually, mainly to make *fufu.* To prepare this thick paste or porridge, the cassava is washed, peeled, boiled, and pounded with mortar and pestle.

> In Brazil, a superior variety of cassava called *mandiba* is ground extra fine and pressed to become the beginnings of tapioca— the dish we are most familiar with in the United States. Tapioca comes from another group of indigenous people, the South American Tupi-Guarani people, who call it *tipioca*.

> Sweet cassava is also widely used and, unlike bitter cassava, does not require a detoxification process. It is eaten raw, like melon, kiln-dried, or cooked.

> In Brazil, a sustainable automobile fuel is being made from sugar, acetone, alcohol, and cassava.

— SP☆TLIGHT—

Ginger *(Zingiber officinale)*

Ginger root varies in size and is a warm yellowish-tan color with a thin skin that is easily peeled. Ginger is pungent, warming, and valuable for its stimulating action that affects the circulation and heart, bringing warmth and well-being. Hot ginger tea promotes perspiration, brings down fever, helps clear catarrh, acts as an expectorant, aids digestion, stimulates appetite, reduces pain, promotes menstruation, treats delayed periods, and deters menstrual clotting, spasms, and painful ovulation. It is also a blood thinner shown to reduce cholesterol and blood pressure. Ginger is used to treat nausea, vomiting, aches, rheumatism, and nervousness. It is a proven nausea/motion sickness remedy that matches or, in some cases, surpasses the drug Dramamine. It thwarts and prevents migraines, headaches, and osteoarthritis, and relieves the symptoms of rheumatoid arthritis.

Ginger is shredded and used as tea, taken in capsule form, used as a food additive/spice, and used decoratively and magickally, whole and dried in potpourri or placed in mojo bags. The types used for the ground ginger we buy as a spice are grown primarily in Jamaica,

Nigeria, and Sierra Leone where ginger is used to flavor curry, stews, and baked goods and to make ginger beer.

Parts used: root and rhizome

Constituents: volatile oil (borneol, cineole, phellandrene, zingiberol, zingiberene)

Properties: antiseptic, diaphoretic, expectorant, digestive antioxidant, circulatory stimulant, hypotensive, decongestant, carminative, rubefacient, antithrombotic, anti-inflammatory, antibiotic (can kill salmonella and staph infection in specific concentrations), antiulcer in animals, antidepressant, antidiarrheal, and strong antioxidant. Ginger also ranks very high in anticancer activity.

Contraindications: Ginger is not recommended for those who suffer from gastritis or peptic ulcers, or those intolerant to heat.

America's Healing Roots

Roots are a cultural bombshell; they are our place of origin both before and after the Middle Passage. We can be grounded, and this type of centering also refers back to the word "root." Much work by contemporary African American health writers, including this one, constantly point back to the roots of our culture as rural. It should not be surprising that those who know how to "heal" with roots in the United States are called *rootworkers*. As we have done some botanical, cultural, conceptual, ceremonial, ritualistic, and philosophic digging in this chapter, in the next there will be space to roll up your sleeves and begin planning and preparing your own sacred spot on Earth.

CHAPTER 7

REWARDING NATURALLY: SACRED SPACES

ven though I did not grow up in a thickly forested section of central Africa, I do share ancestry with the Democratic Republic of Congo's pygmy forest people and Bantu-speaking hunter gatherers of the southeast, so I naturally feel a deep connection to the people there. We have a mutual admiration for the forest. Where I grew up, it was apparent to me that the woods around me, South Jersey's Pine Barrens, had a purpose, and there was an implied sense of ownership of many of the wooded areas. One always wondered whose wood one had stumbled into. Was it hunting season? Were the particular woods one found oneself in safe? Visually, wooded tracts and strands of bushy trees deterred erosion, cattle migrations, and possibly even intruders. I quickly realized the wood was a fixed space with boundaries. I always felt the trees immediately around me, working in concert as a safety shield, as surely as family connection or the comfort zone of a woolen blanket.

In both Africa and the New World, trees play a central role in designing, designating, and demarking space and are as clear and delineating to the informed and initiated as a white picket or barbed wire fence. The first part of this chapter explores the phenomenon in Africa and the New World of sacred groves—collections of trees or entire forests that are dedicated to ancestors or specific deities. We begin by visiting a few of the great sacred groves of Africa and the diaspora, exploring them from a sociopolitical, geographic, magico-spiritual, and philosophic lens. This chapter ends with suggestions for ways of conceptualizing your own sacred space in the form of a garden.

Honoring Trees and Forests

West Africa has so many lessons to teach us. There, the Yoruba people intentionally create wooded areas, called sacred groves, in honor of specific deities. These enclosed, consecrated spaces are fit for use by ancestral spirits as well because they are safe, protected, and indigenous to the area. Some of these spaces are called *Igboro-Egun*, which means "Grove of the Ancestors." Another type of grove also exists. This alternate grove is designed to celebrate specific Orishas; for example, *Igboro-Osayin* is a sacred grove dedicated to Osayin, whom we have discussed previously as Orisha of the Wood and Herbal Magick. You can tell these are sacred places by the trees that occupy their space. Igboro-Egun, for example, hosts *omiyolo, iporogun,* and *atori,* which are some of the Yoruba's most sacred trees/shrubs.

In many traditional African cultures, respect is paid to the spirits of trees during ceremony and ritual. There are special dances performed at designated times of the year to pay tribute to specific plants, trees, resources, and natural spaces, as well as what we consider the designing of "arts and crafts-" like masks and costumes, all to honor the very large group of living and spiritual beings that we place under an umbrella term "nature."

In the first chapter, I discussed the wonder of tree whispering and Jiridon (the science of the trees). Such activities are embraced in Africa and the diaspora, not only by shamans but also by hunters, warriors, healers, artists, and most likely avid gardeners.

Groups of people of African descent pay homage to trees and their attendant spirits differently. For example, in some groups, before cutting down a tree, it is thought that one must address tree spirits, which can be good, bad, neutral, or confused by nature. Acknowledging these types of spirits encourages them to stay in their selected spaces rather than moving into the human domestic space. Disturbing without respect brings bad or confused energy into the household or even into specific individuals in the home. Therefore, it is important to maintain a boundary between certain trees and domestic space, a concept well understood in Africa and the Caribbean. This is especially true when it comes to the tamarind, one of the African diaspora's most spirit-oriented fruit trees. Tamarind, being especially hospitable to spirits, must be treated with ultimate respect when planted near the home.

Over centuries, indigenous Africans have lived close to their environment. Their holistic, traditional, scientific knowledge, which is drawn from experimentation, observation, and innovation, continues to evolve. Taboos, based on spirituality and traditional value systems, have protected the biodiversity of various communities in Africa.

Tree Shelter for "Those who refuse the master"

Trees serve as sanctuary for many different groups of African people under diverse circumstances. There are, for example, the Bamana people, and the Maroons.

> The Bamana people, also called the Minianka, live in a southeastern circle of Koutiala and Yorosso, between Bani and Banifing River. The Minianka subgroup of the Senufo people lives in southeastern Mali or Côte d'Ivoire or northwest

Burkina Faso. Minianka means "Those who refuse the master,"[1] and refers to the fact that fierce warriors of the area would not relinquish their land or freedom during the French conquest. This group's spirituality is intimately tied to nature and to sacred groves.

> Throughout African and African American history there have been people who have sought refuge in the woods from enslavement or other heinous aggressions. "Maroons" are a well-known group who, shortly after enslavement, in places like Suriname or Brazil, quickly found freedom from slavery by taking up residence in the forest.

Firstborn Tree Grove

In addition to the manner in which sacred groves are used to set up geopolitical safety nets and spiritual boundaries from outside influences, there is a fascinating custom by people of Fienso and Minianka villages—the idea of "the firstborn tree grove." This small grove is anchored by a central tree called "firstborn." The people of these types of villages believe trees and plants have ancestors and a soul, just like humans. Firstborn, then, is the first plant of the creator God, called Kle, and it is ancestor of all other plants of the area.

Entire groves exist to offer sanctuary for the firstborn tree. Only the most esteemed initiates know exactly which plant is firstborn, as it is shrouded in secrecy. Most often no one can enter the sacred wood carrying anything harmful to trees, such as metal, an ax, or matches. Because some also believe evil spirits are sheltered in the wood by specific trees, it is likewise considered unsafe to enter the forest without a spiritual guide.

FIRSTBORN TREE RULES

Severe punishments are dispensed to anyone who dares disturb the growth or habit of the firstborn tree of the sacred grove.2

If the sacred wood burns, it is considered a very bad omen for the entire community.

If such a catastrophe occurs, a great effort needs to be made to save the firstborn tree so that its role as ancestor to the forest is preserved, allowing the area to continue to thrive.3

Sacred Grove of the Malshegu Community of Ghana

Malshegu, situated on the Savanna, is located in the northern administration region of Ghana, with five thousand people living there. The settled area came into existence as a way to escape the oppression and rule of Arab invaders from the Sudano-Sahelian region. The Malshegu people are members of the Dagbani ethnic group, and their migration began after the fall of the great empires of ancient Ghana of the twelfth century.

The Malshegu people set aside 0.8 hectares of existing open canopy of forest for their god, Kpalevorgu. Kpalevorgu appears in the form of a boulder, living underneath a large baobab tree. The Malshegu believe that Kpalevorgu's baobab tree helped families over the years, protecting them from invaders. The grove has its own priest, called *Kumbriyili,* who is also a village leader. As the god's sanctuary, this area offers respite from daily goings-on, providing both peace and quiet to those who visit it. It also offers a vantage point for an aerial perspective of the village.

The Malshegu Sacred Grove is one of few remaining examples of a non-riverine, closed-canopy forest in Ghana's savanna. Malshegu Sacred Grove and the god Kpalevorgu's land form part of a rich and complex traditional form of nature conservancy. The grove is a vital habitat, preserving much of the area's fauna and flora, as well as forming physical foci for Malshegu spirituality.

Malshegu Women Farmers

The people have maintained sacred groves, surrounded by Guinea savanna.

Women do most of the tending of the crops, like elsewhere in Africa.

They use animal manure to assure soil fertility, crop rotation, and intercropping with legumes, allowing six months for fallow periods.

Women use hoes and animal traction to prepare the soil.

Chemical fertilizers and pesticides are seldom used.

The sacred grove is an important location for seeds and seed dispersers, which are vital to local cultivation practices. Home to numerous medicinal herbs as well as trees and plants, it has important social and religious functions. The grove ensures that the water table remains high in the immediate area. A baobab tree anchoring the grove indicates a localized high water table. The forest protects Malshegu from wind, rain, storms, brushfires, and potential flooding, and the sacred grove provides an example of ways that traditional societies combine religious and cultural practices, leading to successful environmental and resource management and preservation.[4]

Some Sacred Trees of the New World

Members of specific African tree societies were inevitably brought to the New World and forced to work the land. Some of these Africans came to be known as Gullah people, and it is their labor that produced the famous "Carolina Gold" rice. The Gullah community retains the unique customs of their West African roots, and their language has preserved features of their original tongue, which so many other peoples of the diaspora have lost.

After a lynching, people who had the caul (a gift for seeing into the spirit realm) saw spirits around certain trees, including Angel Oak. Deeply religious, the Gullah call these visions *spirit angels*, and prayers, spiritual offerings, and petitions are made around such trees. This is a common practice among some of our people in the Motherland, as well as elsewhere in the diaspora.

Angel Oak

On Johns Island, South Carolina, which is near Charleston, there is a huge serpentine live oak called Angel Oak. Live oaks spread, rather than grow upward, so the tree is sixty-five feet tall and 160 feet wide, creating 17,100 square feet of shade beneath it. The tree branches go underground and resurface, lending it the distinctive air of a grove of trees, though in reality it is just one tree. Angel Oak predates the planter family for which it was named. It is the oldest tree east of the Mississippi. Having begun its life during the time of King Arthur, Angel Oak is believed to be more than fourteen hundred years old.[5] The tree is purportedly haunted by the souls of enslaved African Americans and those who were lynched on the tree.

Angel Oak can be visited free of charge. If the song hauntingly sung by Billie Holiday, "Strange Fruit," makes your spirit ache, perhaps you should go pay homage to the spirits of enslaved and lynched black folk by making a discreet herbal offering or libation (poured spirit blessing) at Angel Oak.

Lessons of the Trees

Clearly, in Africa and the New World, trees are commanding cultural reservoirs, forming borders and vessels of culture. In Africa, the firstborn tree is the seat of a community. The community grows and thrives along with that tree. Its roots feed on spiritual strength and traditional values. The baobab is a gathering place and shield, supplying food and water to diverse communities. Individual trees and groves are sacred because of their ability to shield, keeping out invaders while germinating medicinal seeds, pods, mosses, ferns, bark, and fungi. The sacred grove is home to insects, birds, reptiles, and animals, as well as divine spirits and ancestors. Angel Oak, the sacred groves of the Yoruba, and numerous other woods have ecological as well as social and religious functions in community health that cannot be underestimated. Sacred groves are a traditional African way of instilling and sustaining biodiversity. Encouraging, honoring, respecting, and protecting healing groves is both African custom and collective responsibility for our future.

Sacred Garden for Conjuration

I love gardening, but as the lessons of the sacred groves teach, tending plants is an opportunity for growing more than fruits, vegetables, flowers, and trees in a mundane way. In gardening each year, I learn a little more about my "self" and the environment, community, state, region, ancestors, and deities that surround me. I call these activities two things: sacred gardening and conjuration. Together they help me build a sacred garden for conjuration, an activity I would like to share with you.

I am a sacred gardener. Through this activity I have gained pleasure, sensual delight, and metaphysical insights. I've even witnessed a miracle or two. My sacred garden draws energy from the sun and water but also, just as important, from daily spiritual practice—prayer, meditation, yoga, rituals, and ceremonies.

Spiritual Terms

Sacred–set apart for worship or veneration; space devoted entirely to a specific purpose; regarding religious objects, rites, or spiritual practice.

Conjure–to summon using supernatural power; to influence or effect by metaphysical means.

Conjuring Spaces

A conjurer's space is somewhat different from a sacred grove. It is typically a space open to oracular animals and prophetic insects, and spiritual objects such as wind chimes, bells, coins, bottles, sea glass, charged rocks, and statuary, along with symbolic flowers and trees designed to invoke energy and presence of specific types. This desirable energy includes ancestors, nature spirits, and deity, as well as varied orders of beings, such as angels. By conjuring energy in a garden space, knowing the language of flowers, trees, and certain deities and elementals, a magickal garden is easily within your reach.

Seeds, bulbs, and eggs are prevalent objects and are harbingers of spring. These symbols help us understand this as the time of great potential. It is time for tilling soil, revealing hidden secrets, dusting off memories and organizing our lives. We try to meet the promise of spring while listening to the almost imperceptible messages of the earth.

Cultivating Wealth of the Greenest Type

When considering sacred gardening, the act of planting seeds is a metaphysical and physical activity. Growth of herbs, flowers, trees, and other plants render opportunities to cultivate many qualities within the self. As you set out to create your gardening space, consider ways that you might:

> Grow patience.

> Set aside time for harvest plans and growth journaling.

> Become acutely aware of local climate changes and conditions in your biome, learning the quirks of your region's meaning of "season."

> Observe the night skies while contemplating your place in the universe.

> Get to know the moon's cycles and how they relate to the act of planting and harvesting.

> Learn to look to the future, striving to envision a sacred space from which you can conjure powerful dreams, visions, healing medicine, and inspiration.

> Sketch your garden's growth without self-consciousness or judging (this is liberating).

> Embrace beauty in all its forms.

> Use your garden as an opportunity to beautify your home while contributing to the holistic health of your neighborhood by using indigenous planting techniques that lessen your ecological footprint.

> Welcome the fruits of your labor and share them with human, animal, deity, spirits, the ancestors, and even beasts (if you know any).

Beginning Your Work: Consider a Tribute to Elegba

Many West African ceremonies or rituals begin with an offering to the deity Elegba to ensure success. Identified with Saint Anthony and Saint Michael, Elegba's colors can be red and black or black and white. His symbolic *caminos* or paths to knowing him, which are comparable to Western avatars, are canes, staffs, and pipes.

To begin your conjuring garden, it is important to honor Elegua (Lucumi), also called Eshu or Elegba (Yoruba-inspired traditions of Candomblé and Santeria), Exus or Exuas (Umbanda and Quimbois), and Legba and Papa Legba (Vodou). This deity or group of deities probably originated with Yoruba people but spread throughout the African diaspora.

Elegba owns the crossroads of one's life and controls fortune and misfortune. He also represents death, an integral element of the wheel and planting season. As a trickster, Elegba can present difficult options during vision quest. It is wise to devise a way of paying tribute with appropriate colors, plants, and treats specific to Elegba before beginning your sacred garden. Do this reverently at the nearest crossroads to your house.

Charging Rocks

Esu is a Yoruban concept representing the spiritual energy rising out of *Yangi*, "sacred red rock," which allows communication with Orisha Orunmila.

You'll probably want to include Esu for conjure gardening as well. Esu lives in consecrated rocks. Often I use charged river rocks to honor Esu. I also honor Orisha Oshun because she is specific to the rivers, water banks, fresh water, beauty, and the arts. I invoke her energy while honoring her by placing river rocks and pea pebble in the garden.

To charge rocks means to transform them from mundane to sacred healing objects. There are a couple of ways of doing this:

1. Bury and then unearth them. If they feel lighter and warmer, they are charged; if not, repeat the process until they are.

2. Soak rocks under the full moon in a consecrated substance such as rose or lavender water or even saltwater. Do this for seven days. Remove and sun-dry the rocks. If they feel lighter or denser or you detect any significant changes, they are charged and ready to use.

Horseshoe on House or Tree

Next, you need to consider ways of adding good luck to your venture. For this, many African Americans have depended upon the powers of Ogun, metal Orisha and warrior, placing some form of him in or near the home. You might also want to place a  horseshoe on your property on or near your garden with veneration, focus, and intent. The horseshoe embodies the energy of warrior Orishas and gods of protection such as Ogun. This set of gods is associated with metallurgy and metalsmithing. Even for tribes and language groups other than the Yoruba, metal and its transformation are revered. During early African American history and that of the Freed Men, metalsmithing was a coveted and well-respected trade. Metallic objects such as a horseshoe pay tribute to African metalsmithing while adding an important layer of shielding and protection around the garden.

Proper Horseshoe Use

To catch the good luck, place your horseshoe with the cup shape facing upward; otherwise you are simply catching and spilling away abundance.

Whitewashed Fence or Tree

You often see a whitewashed fence or tree on southern African American property though it also exists elsewhere. Why white? To examine one concept articulated by the Yoruba, in holistic healing, white represents one of the most important bodily and spiritual functions. White represents the "other world," that is, the spirit world, from which we conjure energy. The color and concept called *funfun* in Yorubaland is a metaphysical designation; it is possible for spirits of many kinds (animal, spiritual, natural, and elemental), ancestors, and humans to interact in this conceptual zone. A whitewashed fence around the garden or a whitewashed tree on your property is a way to cultivate this potent West African idea, affording the opportunity to engage and harvest "white spirit world" energy.

Garden as Spirit-Animal Sanctuary

Your created space can potentially attract and retain the energy of physical and spiritual creatures beneficial to your garden, enhancing its overall desirability and spirituality. You can create a symbolic sanctuary, first by understanding the symbolism of wildlife, and then by attracting certain types of creatures.

Ants—Welcome ants to your garden and leave appropriate offerings in front of anthills to be carried off to spirit world. Ants are capable of forging a road between human, ancestor, and spirit, and working with ants is an immediate and fun way to begin crossing over into the spirit realm from the garden space. A visit from army ants is considered a blessing and signifies the need for more offerings.

Bees—Bees are symbolic of fertility, renewal, and fecundity. Mande people consider bees harbingers of blessings and associate them with longevity; getting stung is considered lucky. Your garden won't go very far without bees, so make the space pleasing to them by planting flowers and bushes attractive to them, such as bee balm flowers.

Birds—Birds appear to touch and disappear into the heavens and are therefore thought to be spiritual messengers and spirit animals. Believed to take offerings and sacrifices to ancestors, deities, or spirits, birds are watched and listened to closely—admired as some of the animal kingdom's best oracles. Birds are intermediaries between humans and divinities; they carry spiritual wisdom on their wings. Birds' presence in the garden suggests sustainability, stability, safety, and life. It is wise to have bird feeders and a birdbath in or near your garden to welcome these heavenly creatures.

Crocodile—Brokers of power and mystical forces with great energy, crocodile is also an oracle. Crocodile jaws symbolize the ability to consume negative energy; they represent water spirit and collect sacrifices and offerings left in moving water. Crocodile is celebrated because it carries sacrifices to ancestors and spirits through bodies of water. Crocodile is respected as a formidable physical specimen and metaphysical force—images of crocs on tiles, statues, bowls, or woven rugs should be added to the conjurer's garden so that it becomes a place where oracular messages can be received.

Mouse/Rat—Though they've gotten a bad rap in American society, mice and rats are highly respected by several African groups who believe that, because of their natural closeness to the earth, mice and rats have metaphysical powers and can even serve as oracles. According to folklore, these reviled rodents once had the ability to speak, making them effective messengers of natural and supernatural knowledge. Mice can be made to feel welcome in the flower garden with food offerings like seeds or nuts.

Porcupine—Porcupine quill is a symbol of brave warrior and generally refers to weaponry, suggesting the ability to ward off evil sorcery. Porcupine is considered a wise animal in West Africa so, as such, welcome porcupine quills into sacred spaces like your garden as symbols of intelligence. Porcupine quills, statues, plaques, woven cloth, and quills can be added to the garden.

Snakes—Qualities of snake that are admired are its ability to survive on land and in water, its ability to camouflage itself and blend quietly into its environment, its ability to hunt and eat much larger, more powerful prey than itself, and its venom, which demonstrates very strong *nyama* (nature as a sacred whole). In Haiti's Vodou, Damballah is the eldest and chief of the Lwa (intermediary spirits akin to angels). Damballah is a primordial serpent deity who created our planet and the deities who rule it. He is of such antiquity that he does not even need to speak to be heard; like DNA, he is at the core of our being. Damballah Hwedo and his wife, Ayedo Hwedo, should be welcomed in the garden. They appreciate offerings of white things, especially eggs.

Toad—Looked upon as a mystical creature because transformation is a part of its core being (as evidenced by its profound maturation from the tadpole to its adult manifestation as the toad), it also aids healers' spiritual work with forest medicine.

Turtle/Tortoise—The turtle represents the feminine and is called upon in fertility rites. As creatures of land and water, turtles are considered quite adaptable and smart. Turtle and tortoise are in the shape-shifter spirit animal family, meaning they can change into other animal forms at will.

For many in more urban environments, it makes sense to have symbolic animals in the garden. Most of the animals discussed can be represented as figures that are made from stoneware and fired so they are weatherproof. They can also be represented in tiles or, if you're crafty, set out in mosaic patterns. Outlets specializing in

African symbolism (such as *sacredsource.com*) sell sacred icons as statuary. Make sure whatever you select is weatherproof.

Dressing for Natural Power

Seed magick has a venerable African history, recorded back to the Fifth Dynasty of Egypt, where bodies were found adorned with seed necklaces. Wearing seed jewelry is important while planting. In ancient Khemet, such jewelry was used against evil on mummified bodies and worn by the living to ward off illness. One of the most important plants you can draw from is Job's tears *(Coix lacryma-jobi)*, also called prayer seeds. Harkening back to a Congolese healer's art called "medicine string," Job's tears are a species of grass (Maydeae family). The plant's fruit suggests a seed. The plant grows in marshes and has a place in "Secret Doctor" medicine, used as an amulet for protection and prayer; in Hoodoo, it is used as a wishing bean.

Beads can also play a part; to create your garden and plant your hopes, carry three concealed beads for luck and throw seven beads in a freshwater source.

Stoking the Conjure's Garden

Now that we have the animal spirits' attention (as well as that of powerful deities), it's time to consider the planting itself. You can look in Richter's Catalog or online suppliers to find seeds of these plants, essentials for the conjurer's garden:

Deer's tongue *(Frasera speciosa, Liatris odoratissima)* has a scent similar to vanilla and is thought of as a lust-inducing, aphrodisiac herb that also helps quell gossip.

Devil's shoestring *(Viburnum alnifolium)* is a stringy barked stick that is used to help get you out of trouble.

High John the Conqueror root *(Ipomoea jalapa, I. purga)* embodies the spirit of a heroic, courageous, fearless survivor of slavery. Carrying this magickal root on your person in a mojo bag (made from a piece of red flannel) or sprinkling the powder from it on your money is thought to bring good fortune.

Queen Elizabeth root or orris root *(Iris florentina)* yields an inviting, tempting, attractive root, which is pulverized and used in love-binding formulas. In ancient Khemet, the scent and power of the iris (Queen Elizabeth) was considered to be strong enough to transform any other plant with which it came into contact. In Hoodoo, Queen Elizabeth root is believed to enhance the power of individual herbs and generally strengthen any mojo or potion to which it is added.

Rose *(Rosa spp.)* enhances the spiritual frequency of the sacred garden. When selecting potential roses, seek out the old-fashioned scented types rather than the more neutral tea roses. Roses are beautiful and, like the lotus, they suggest female genitalia at the height of passion. The blush of the rose is often likened to the blush of a bride or a sexual partner during orgasm. In parts of Africa and the Middle East, holy temples are spiritually cleansed with highly potent Bulgarian rosewater.

Poetry of Plants

When you close your eyes and visualize your magickal garden, I'm sure it is now filled with intriguing conjure plants, images of oracular animals, auspicious insects, and mystical birds. Your mind may also reverberate with a rainbow of colors, intricate shapes, and alluring fragrances of herbs and flowers. When choosing flowers for the conjurer's garden, refer to this passage derived from the extensive Victorian Language of Flowers to find out what each flower, tree, and organic fertilizer represents:

Algae—good fortune, prosperity (and seaweed used as a fertilizer).

Balm of Gilead *(Commiphora opobalsamum* [preferable], *Cedronella canariensis)*—has been an important spiritual flower to African Americans for hundreds of years for its connection to spirituality and as a powerful metaphor of survival.

Bergamot *(Citrus aurantium var. bergamia)*—inspires confidence, gives energy.

Blood—an important magickal and practical substance, used as a libation for good fortune; such as goat's blood, which is used both for sacrificial work and fertilizer.

Calendula *(Calendula officinalis)*—brings brightness, success, and well wishes.

Daisy *(Chrysanthemum leucanthemum* or *Bellis perennis)*—speaks of true love unfettered by appearances; it says: "You are my real first love."

Forget-me-not *(Myosotis sylvatica)*—reminds the receiver that they are not forgotten.

Gardenia *(Gardenia augusta)*—beloved by African American southern gardeners, gardenia is one of the only perfectly balanced scents around, containing a top note (one of the first things you smell in a blended perfume or cologne) as well as the middle and base note; can be worn in the hair, placed near the bed, or carried in a bouquet.

Hollyhock *(Althaea rosea)*—symbolizes fertility: "I am fertile, how about you?"

Honeysuckle *(Lonicera caprifolium)*—refers to a plea for commitment, as if to say, "This is it—let's get hitched."

Iris *(Iridaceae)*—represents strength.

Jasmine *(Jasminum officinale)*—a romantic flower, also like a narcotic, easing stress and anxiety.

Lemon verbena *(Lippia citriodora)*—a symbol of attraction, suggesting, "I am excited and mesmerized by you."

Lily *(Liliaceae)*—represents purity.

Mango *(Mangifera)*—conjures fertility, community, and harmonious family relationships.

Meadowsweet *(Filipendula ulmaria)*—also called brideswort, a traditional flower given to brides for luck and to calm their nerves.

Orange blossom *(Citrus sinesis)*—draws commitment; can be grown indoors or outside.

Red carnation *(Dianthus caryophyllus)*—a flower of passion suggesting, "This love is really hot!"

Red tulip *(Tulipa spp.)*—a direct-speaking flower, says simply, "I love you."

Roses *(Rosa spp.)*—represent sensuality, beauty, and joy.

Tobacco leaf *(Nicotana)*—sends salutations to the ancestors, family, and community.

Indigenous Tree Energy

For shade, wisdom, inspiration, and medicine, you'll want to situate your garden near a tree. Pine, holly, and oak renew and empower us in the wood, in the home, and in our bodies.

Here are some trees that grow well in most regions of the United States.

Holly *(Ilex)*: Holly's deep green leathery leaves and bright red or white berries brighten the spirits. Holly has numerous recorded uses among early African Americans along the southeast coast, particularly in Gullah medicine. They are well-appreciated trees during winter celebrations of Yule and its later relative Christmas.

Conifers (evergreens): Evergreens are a metaphor for the interaction between departed spirits and their living community. Pine *(Pinus spp.)* and spruce *(Picea spp.)* trees in particular play a key role in traditional African American burials in the southern United States. Also consider adding black spruce, fir, or juniper.

Black spruce—with its mellow, deep woods scent

Cedarwood—spiced evergreen, deep and powerful

Fir—somewhat brighter and sharper needles than cedar, but not acrid

Juniper—berry mixed with evergreen

Further Afield

Some consider the following exotics; it all depends on where you live. These are venerable trees with known magickal qualities, so if it is at all possible, have one or more of these in your garden. Some, such as banana, orange, and pineapple, can be wintered indoors in temperate zones and taken out in pots during the spring, summer, and warmer parts of fall.

Banana *(Musa spp.)*—Along with fig, coconut, and tamarind, the banana is one of the most important cross-cultural African spiritual trees; good for indoor or outdoor gardening in warm conditions. The leaf is used to ensure fertility and encourage both vitality and good health.

Coconut *(Cocos nucifera)*—a tree of love; myriad symbols in African belief systems, including cleansing, purity, greetings to the gods, goddesses, and ancestral spirits.

Fig *(Ficus carica)*—symbolic of fidelity and chastity; a good indoor tree specimen from *Ficus spp.* can be brought outdoors in warm conditions.

Magnolia *(Magnolia acuminate; M. virginiana)*—of love goddess and planet Venus; in Hoodoo, a few magnolia leaves under the bed, mattress, or pillows is thought to ensure fidelity.

Mango *(Mangifera)*—conjures fertility, community, and smooth family relationships.

Orange *(Citrus sinesis)*—orange blossoms draw commitment; the tree can be grown indoors or outside.

Sweet myrtle *(Myrtus communis)*—considered the top love-draw herb, and helps conjure fidelity and joyful relationships; can be worn by a bride with a veil or carried as part of the bridal bouquet.

Tamarind *(Tamarindus indica)*—a tree of love, sensuality, sharing, strong magick, and community.

Plant Lwa

Vodou is an awe-inspiring tradition of bringing together plant energy with divinity, spiritual, and personal energy. It affirms the relationships of cycles of life, nature, ancestors, and spirits. Vodou's vision of spirits understands them as the intelligence of energy present in humans, nature, and thoughts.

Mysteries can be understood through spirits known on this path as Lwa. Lwa are intermediaries between Bondye (very remote,

Pineapple Tree (Bromeliaceae)

Another magickal and venerable exotic tree is the pineapple tree. It is easy to grow from a pineapple fruit top. Cut off, leave a little of the fruit, remove the lower leaves, and let dry for a few days. Put in water until roots appear. Plant in a pot in potting soil, and you'll have your own pineapple tree. In Puerto Rico and elsewhere, this tree represents friendly greetings and convivial warmth.

omnipotent God) and humans. The Lwa were once mortals and share some human characteristics, for better or worse, including strength, vision, ego, capriciousness, and fickle emotions; they can be demanding and sometimes tricky. Two that you want to salute with your sacred garden efforts are:

Gran Bwa—This Lwa helps you connect to ancestral roots or the spiritual home of Vodou. Offerings of basins of water, leaves, roots, branches, or flowers are welcomed. A drawing of the tree of life is a good conduit to Gran Bwa. A tree sapling can be planted on Gran Bwa's behalf. Gran Bwa energy exists at each magickal point of every tree. Ask Gran Bwa to enter heart, arm, and legs through a ritual dance on your tilled soil.

Gran Ibo—Those who find magick and wisdom in the swamp and its plants need to know Gran Ibo, Lwa of swamps. She understands the language of plants and is holder of ancient plant knowledge—all the way from its roots because that is where knowledge is held. Everything natural—trees, roots, leaves, pods, flowers, bark, insects, animals, bird, and reptiles—all find their way through difficulty by attuning to wisdom held by Gran Ibo. Sacred swamp plants and trees include lotus, orchid, swamp oak, sandalwood, and magnolia.

Water Features: Bringing It All Together

I saved the best for last. One of the most important ways you can make your garden sacred and capable of conjuration is through water and water features. Water has an important seat in African diasporic magick. In Hoodoo, we utilize sacred waters in baths, blessings, soaks, libations, teas, floor washes, on the altar, and more. In your conjurer's garden, this translates into waterfalls, birdbaths, koi or turtle ponds, and appreciation of rain.

I recommend collecting rain and lightning water in barrels or buckets to be used to feed your seedlings and saplings. Rain usually brings more gentle energy of the female fertility deities, whereas lightning water brings change, swiftly ushering in transformation. In South Africa among chiShona speakers, rain is seen as the manifestation of the sacred queens, the Mujajis. These queens, goddesses in the flesh as it were, are responsible for fertility, growth, development, and fruitful yield. They must always be honored, especially around planting and growing situations. Pay tribute to the Mujajis with your quiet praise songs and graceful moves. Utilize the Mujajis' precious gifts to help your sacred garden develop the ability to conjure and, at the same time, help the earth.

Sacred Gardens for Everyone

Having a sacred space, whether an entire grove you can tend and visit or a conjurer's sacred garden, will enlighten and bring endless creative thoughts as well as sensual pleasures.

Metaphysical sacred spaces are for tilling, planning, discovering, sorting, envisioning, dreaming, and meditating. Sacred-earth tending provides an area to deepen spiritual connection with plants, wildlife, the elements, deity, and yourself. These are your spaces for learning more about yourself and those around you—great, small, and invisible—with the guidance of Mother Nature.

Even the most urban dweller or those without a green thumb can be refreshed by visiting a local conservatory or nearby forest preserve. Small spaces like apartments, condos, and even dorm rooms can host different sorts of trees and plants: windowsill herb gardens and banana, kumquat, lemon, palm, and fig trees grow well indoors and can be clipped back so as not to take enormous amounts of space. I should know; I live in a converted two-flat in an urban suburb with limited space for outdoor gardening. When it comes to getting in touch with the sacred nature of gardening, it isn't size that matters; it is the intent in your heart and the spaces you allow in your soul.

CHAPTER 8

A FRESH START: HOLISTIC DETOX

D etoxification using a combination of baths, steam, salt, and herbs is an ancient African healing tradition that has been passed down and spread through the diaspora. Whereas many consider detox a concern of the body, in this chapter I examine the practice of holistic detox, which is detoxification of the mind, body, and spirit as a unit. Unlike invasive, unpleasant methods of detoxification such as enemas, this chapter shares gentle herbal techniques that cleanse safely and effectively.

Although my work is usually all about building bridges between modalities, methodologies, and cultures, after delving deeply into African holistic medicine, African derived religions (ADRs), and African traditional religions (ATRs), I see a significant disconnection between Western herbal medicine and the healing ways of the Motherland and diaspora. At one time, herbs were part of an integrated, holistic activity that also utilized other significant spiritual tools such as ritual and ceremony. Editing out the spiritual basis of herbalism strips its long-standing connection to earth wisdom and faith.

Today in the West, herbs are "used" to treat body ailments as a quick-fix "cure" or temporary help, much like a pill. But there is so much more to the working of herbs. Ancient Egyptians, Khemetians, and our people from nearby kingdoms such as Ethiopia and Sheba realized that herbs aren't very effective without spiritual agency. Without that, they cease to be a special, holistic treatment for a variety of ailments. This is why herbal medicine is often dispensed as a part of a ceremony or ritual.

Spiritual Term

Spiritual agency—working through or under the auspices of spiritual guides, faith, the ancestors, or other spiritual guidance.

In African holistic health, herbs are not "used" but honored, and they do not stand alone but are part of a complex foundation that includes veneration of the ancestors, deity, spirits, the elements, and ashe. We cannot do all healing on our own, nor can all healing work be done by herbs alone.

The paradigm shift in herbal methodology—from a spiritual to a strictly pragmatic point of view—is largely a result of commercial industries latching onto herbs and hyping their efficacy in a variety of industrial, chemical-laden products. You've seen them in dish detergent, clothes detergent such as Tide (with aloe vera or lavender), and even in Vasoline (with shea butter or aloe vera), a largely fossil-fuel product filled with petroleum. My concern is: What happens to herbs in this mix? How can they operate their magick while mired in chemicals?

Detoxification from a Western herbalism perspective is also big business. There are now even kits for detoxification, especially prominent at New Year's. They include wonderful herbs like dandelion, milk thistle, flaxseed, and parsley. They clean us through our kidneys, liver, and bowels, but toxicity is a much more complex issue.

In many parts of Africa, shamans look for environmental, spiritual, and bodily symptoms when addressing an ailment such as toxicity. In the African diaspora, detoxifications with herbs, baths, or a combination of the two are used to address holistic disorder. This approach is growing in popularity in the West. As a condition that affects our mental state, which can in turn hamper our spirituality, toxicity is of concern as a holistic issue and needs to be treated holistically.

Analysis and Awareness

The most important step in detoxification in a holistic sense is to become aware of mind, body, and spirit. You can cultivate this type of awareness for yourself, family, friends, loved ones, or even clients. Some do it for their animal companions or spirits around them as well—whoever or whatever needs it.

Breath

Because breath comes from deep within one's body, illness, be it of the mind, body, or spirit, emits a smell, usually found on one's breath. Be aware of your breath and that of others in your daily encounters. Scent is important; animals use smell quite a bit to navigate the world and understand what is going on. As animals ourselves, we instinctively know the importance of smell, but because it not much valued in our social world, we forget to pay attention to it.

So many of us can't catch our breath—why is that? In the process of becoming more aware, one of the key issues to consider is breathwork. Toxic people and situations (whether involving friends, foes, loved ones, animals, spirits, or jobs) impact the breath negatively. When absorbing this toxicity, the breath comes shorter and shallower. Shallow breathing has all sorts of negative impacts on your body, from localized aches and pains (cramps, headache, backache, and stomachache) to more general bodily issues such as dizziness, insomnia, infertility, and impotence—all stemming, in part, from lack of oxygen. Holding one's breath too long and not releasing it fully puts internal organs (kidney, liver, heart, pancreas, thyroid, and more) in a constant state of high alert; eventually, they tire and fail to function.

African Yoga

Though many believe yoga with its attendant pranayama (breathing practice) comes from India, others honor it as being rooted in ancient Egypt. African-styled yoga combines four sacred systems of the diaspora, drawn from Vodou, Khemetian, Palo, and Yoruban practices. African yoga is often accompanied by drums and flutes and tends to be very fluid.

Environmental Stressors

What does exposure to toxic people, rocky romantic relationships, tenuous friendships, stressful situations, draining jobs, unstable home environments, dysfunctional family dynamics, and noxious community issues have to do with the necessity for detoxification? African healers know that environmental hazards, human *or* spiritual in nature, can poison us, and cause havoc to our systems in much the same way as toxic chemicals.

Toxic people and situations are like viruses. You may not be sure how you caught them, but the most important issue is how to get rid of them. How much effort does it require and what are the repercussions for your brain, emotions, psyche, spirit, and even your soul if these things are not banished or purged? One of the first steps of action is analysis through holistic awareness (a good African shaman or natural healer can do this analysis), examining every aspect of the environmental situation: mental, spiritual, and physical.

Spiritual Entity Attachment

Toxic people and situations may or may not have spiritual entity attachment. In spiritual entity attachment, needy spirits, bad spirits, or playful and mischievous spirits inhabit the toxic source. You need to be alert to this possibility and you will likely need daily prophylactics—and, no, I'm not talking condoms.

Spiritual prophylactics can be charms, amulets, chants, affirmations, or prayers. This type of prophylactic can stem from many self-determined aspects such as:

> The power of your sacred personal space

> Your mastery of candlemancy

> Your ability to negotiate spirit world through trance, assisted by dance, movement, or sound (djembe and rattles)

The Power Couple in Holism: The Mental and the Spiritual

Healing in a holistic sense—overcoming toxic people, places, or situations—requires strong mental and spiritual work. This is of key significance in detoxification of the mind, body, and spirit.

> Mental capacity must be expanded through awareness.

> Spiritual connections with deva, elemental, deity, nature spirit, spirit guide, and the Creator must all be cultivated and maintained on a daily basis.

> Then the physical self, perhaps the weakest part of the mind-body-spirit trilogy but nevertheless an important part of our life on this Earth, can begin detoxification.

Elemental Detox

As you've seen, elements are very important in African holistic health, particularly the cumulative power that is derived from them. Here are the elements (they're cost-free, by the way) that can play a significant role in holistic detoxification.

1. **Water** is a vital substance for our bodies and, in an African sense, a critical spiritual tool.

2. **Fire** encourages purging and banishment. There is a spiritual route to enlightenment through two simple methods that draw upon fire: incense and candles.

3. **Air** is the element that encourages you to evaluate breath and to correct breathing patterns when necessary.

4. **Earth** invites you to travel, see, touch, lie on, move with, and appreciate the splendor of all seasons and situations. Veneration of the earth—earth magick—can be part of holistic detox.

5. **Akashic energy** encourages you to go outside your physical and spiritual body. Visiting other times and places on vision quests and through dreaming, meeting your team of spirit guides, and divination can all be tremendously important to protection and guidance, awareness building, projecting, attracting positive energy, and eliminating waste from the entire system. These are concepts honored in Africa and various parts of the diaspora by diviners, healers, shamans, and other healing practitioners.

Healing Power of Water

Water is a very healing substance. Pulling it inside our bodies, orally or through the skin, helps flush out toxins. Being submerged in water, swimming or soaking (even soaking particular body parts) in sea salts or minerals and herbs, is a very African way of utilizing the power of water.

Water is seen in many parts of Africa as a layer over the spirit world. This means spirit and ancestors along with certain deities live in or beneath water. Water animals carry offerings to spirit, deity, and ancestors. Deity or elemental mediators can be contacted through the aqueous vehicle of water.

Additional Cleansing Aids

Saunas (wet or dry)
Gentle skin brushing (exfoliation)
Professional lymph-draining massages
Daily showers

Spiritual Detox

Here are some ideas for spiritual detox:

1. **Unhook**—Remove yourself from toxic people or situations, even on a trial basis if necessary.
2. **Retreat**—Retreat into yourself, your room, your home, your mind, your dream world; create a private space to sort things out.
3. **Insulate**—Try to insulate yourself by consuming stimulating herbal teas, soul foods, good books, or enjoyable music. Of course, to achieve similar states of relaxation and insulation,

some people use food, alcohol, drugs, shopping, sex, or religious zeal, but the negatives far outweigh the ephemeral feel-good effect these extreme methods can bring with them.

4. **Expand horizons**—Walk the labyrinth (a labyrinth is a pattern drawn on the earth or created by plants such as hedges that requires meditation and reflection to travel through to the end successfully), create or color mandalas, walk, meditate, strive to meet new people, and travel (dream, astral, or physical).

5. **Make decisions**—Take a leap in your perceived "right direction."

6. **Renew faith**—In whatever way works best, renew faith in yourself and your abilities.

The Powerful Freebies

Some great opportunities to clear mind and spirit include New Year's, the advent of spring, back-to-school, back-to-work, or the fiscal new year. We can embrace and fully utilize these opportunities for rebirth by freely engaging in prayer, meditation, and exercise, and getting a good night's sleep.

Spring-Clearing

During spring-cleaning, which typically begins around Ostara (spring equinox), there is a cleansing or purging of winter's sedentary ways, with a general opening up and airing out of both ourselves and our homes. This allows us to take our place in the Wheel of the Year (earth-based spirituality, pre-Christian [Pagan] holiday observances) and seasonal cycles, and to treat our bodies just as we do the body of Earth and our personal spaces on it (such as those groves and gardens discussed in chapter 7). Simply, we clear the old and make way for new growth.

Living the Good Life

The word "liver" was *lifer* in Old English. You can clearly see in this organ's etymological structure that liver is also "one who lives," attesting to how quintessential it is to our existence.

When talking detox, you're going to start thinking like a liver if, like most people, you desire a full and vibrant lifestyle. Liver, the organ, cleanses and filters the bloodstream. As we saw in chapter 4, the quality of one's blood is very important in African spiritual and health practices. Healers in Africa and in the diaspora are concerned with determining if blood is too thick, too thin, too sweet, or too bitter.

Cod Liver Oil

Cod liver oil helps replenish those who have detoxed. My Aunt Edith, our family wisewoman, insisted that we have a teaspoon of cod liver oil each morning and more when we returned from school, something I hated then but now know provides the body with beneficial omega-3 fatty acids, which help improve both mood and brain function. Moreover, fish oil keeps the heart healthy; just one ounce per day cuts the risk of heart disease by 50 percent. It also fights high blood pressure and rheumatoid arthritis. Cod oil has anti-inflammatory and anticoagulant (blood-thinning) properties.

Another vital function of the liver is to detoxify, metabolize, and transform hazardous substances like ammonia, metabolic waste, drugs, alcohol, and chemicals into tolerable substances. Liver enzymes break down toxic molecules structurally, reducing their toxicity. Liver failure can be a result of: unhealthy diet; alcohol or drug abuse; environmental toxins in the workplace, home, school, or neighborhood; pharmaceuticals (adverse reaction or conflict with other prescriptions); and viral hepatitis. Excess weight gain can sometimes indicate liver dysfunction, especially when you are not overeating. Detoxifying the system can strengthen the liver, helping to ensure that it continues to perform its vital role in our bodies.

Stocking Your Herbal Detox Kit

There are a wide variety of herbs to help you cleanse your liver and tone other internal organs. Here is a solid list of well-respected herbs to help you build a workable Herbal Detox Kit.

Burdock root *(Arctium pubens)*
Burdock root is an unparalleled blood cleanser and detoxifier that speeds the elimination of toxins. This rigorous growing root stimulates digestion and liver action. It has a favorable effect on the pancreas while also strengthening weak digestion. It is a mild diuretic that eases water retention (for this reason, it may cause sweating). The roots, leaves, and seeds are all used medicinally.

Calendula *(Calendula officinalis)*
Calendula is an antiseptic astringent that stimulates the immune system. Hot calendula tea encourages sweating, promotes good

circulation, and helps the body purge toxins. Weak calendula tea also soothes irritations of the stomach lining and bowels, and can also quell diarrhea. However, this herb cannot be used during pregnancy—at all.

Lay Off the Cascara Sagrada

Cascara sagrada *(Rhamnus purshiana):* Decoction of cascara sagrada ("sacred bark" in Spanish) has strong effects on the bowels and stimulates cleansing of the liver, stomach, and pancreas. The warnings for this herb, however, go on and on. It cannot, for example, be used by pregnant or lactating women, and it cannot be used for more than a week at a time. Moreover, it can cause bloody stool, vomiting, and a host of other violent reactions, particularly when combined with contraindicated drugs. If you use this potentially dangerous substance at all, use it sparingly and with discretion.

Dandelion *(Taraxacum officinale)*

Love these little devils. Tenacious, they are the yellow plague of the suburbs—and they don't leave urbanites alone either. Each spring they are anywhere and everywhere. Good thing for us, too, because, like the good weed they are, they suck up all the nutrition they can get from the soil and nearby plants. You can decoct a cleansing tea from the dandelion root. (Of course, you shouldn't take them from roadsides or toxic locales, but anywhere else where it's legal to do so is fine.) Dandelion root stimulates the liver, enabling efficient detoxification. It removes pesticides, pollutants, contaminants, wastes, and toxins that collect in the joints. It cools and cleanses the liver. It also promotes circulation, while strengthening the arteries. Dandelion root is good for the urinary tract and may even help dissolve urinary stones. You can eat the leftover leaves raw as salad or stir-fry as a tender green for additional health benefits.

Flaxseed (Linum catharticum, L. usitatissimum)

Flaxseed is a bulk-forming laxative. When someone is very ill but strong enough to take a good cleansing, flaxseed can be an effective go-to. What I like about flaxseed is that it cleanses the intestines and soothes and rinses the urinary tract, partly due to the phytochemical lignans it contains.

Usage: Crush 2 teaspoons of the seeds in a coffee grinder; blend until fairly fine. Steep in 1 cup of boiled (slightly cooled) water. Strain. Sweeten with honey if desired.

Garlic (Allium sativum L.)

Add crushed garlic to water with lemon and honey (Long Life Juice); also add garlic (hand crushed and finely cut) to eggs, stir-fry, salad, and savory dishes as often as possible.

Ginger (Zingiber officinale)

When cooking or making smoothies, add fresh or powdered ginger. Ginger adds a great deal of energy to your morning drink.

Milk Thistle (Silybum marianum)

Milk thistle tea is used to detoxify the liver when it has been abused by drugs and alcohol. It contains silymarin, a unique combination of flavonolignans that shield the liver cells from damage by free radicals and toxins. Milk thistle is known to:

> Strengthen the liver

> Amp up disease-resistance

> Speed recovery generally and from substance abuse

> Cleanse the blood

> Rid the system of harmful chemicals, pollutants, and wastes

> Encourage the system to secrete bile

> Stimulate digestive juices that break down nutrients from foods, making them easier for cells to absorb and, in the process, dissolving fat-soluble toxins

A month of drinking a cup or two of milk thistle tea daily is usually suggested for full effect in detoxification.

NOTE: Milk thistle is also believed to help the body recover from chemotherapy and radiation.

Parsley *(Apium petroselinum)*

Fresh leaves, roots, and seeds are ingested to cleanse the glands, liver, and gallbladder. I take my parsley as a tea infusion or eat raw with salad.

Plantain *(Plantago major)*

A weed in North America that can be successfully wildcrafted, thus obtained free of charge from your property, plantain successfully removes toxins from the blood.

Turmeric *(Curcuma longa)*

Turmeric contains curcumin, the powerful antioxidant that stimulates the gallbladder and scavenges free radicals. Turmeric is a beloved liver cleaner in Ayurvedic medicine, the ancient medical tradition that originated in India and which has filtered into the communities we share with people of East Indian origins, such as suburbs of New York and New Jersey and various locales in Jamaica and South Africa. As a bitter, turmeric helps cleanse the liver and purify blood, cultivates proper digestion, and facilitates elimination of waste. It also protects the gallbladder and stimulates circulation. It is a powerful anti-inflammatory without the adverse side effects of most anti-inflammatory drugs.

Turmeric is a warming spice, a thermogenic, which means it boosts metabolism. Cinnamon, cumin, black pepper, red peppers, chilies, and cayenne are other thermogenic foods and spices. Add them to soups or stews for multiple benefits. Having an efficiently tuned metabolism yields surprising health benefits. You feel light and warm in the mind, body, and spirit, and as long as you watch portion sizes, these thermogenic foods can also help you lose weight. Additionally, they can increase energy, stamina, and focus, which is also helpful for the short days and long nights of winter.

Turmeric has a further action conducive to weight loss. Like dandelion root and milk thistle, it is lipotropic.

Lipotropic herbs and whole foods encourage fat to exit the liver, which facilitates the metabolizing of fat.

Recommendation: Buy whole turmeric pieces and grind them in a mortar and pestle or coffee bean grinder to gain maximum nutrient potential. If unavailable, buy pre-ground; in the pursuit of medicinal qualities, the fresher the better (check expiration dates).

Warning: Turmeric is a possible irritant, allergen, and sensitizer; contraindicated for those with congestive heart failure.

Yarrow *(Achillea millefolium)*

Yarrow is a superb blood purifier and really gets the circulation going. In the digestive system, it helps fight inflammation and infections in the stomach lining and intestines. It contains bitters, which help tone the digestive tract. Yarrow is exceedingly easy to grow and makes an appealing floral show. A multi-use herb, yarrow is particularly recommended for cleansing the body internally.

Cleaning Up Your Act

It may seem self-evident, but during periods of detoxification it is hoped that you will stop or limit whatever harmful activity may have sparked the desire for cleansing. It is suggested that you reduce or eliminate your intake of red meat, dairy products, poultry, wheat, black tea, coffee, and citrus fruit, and that you concentrate instead on raw or steamed vegetables, whole grains (other than wheat), nuts, and non-citrus fruits (particularly pineapple). As a general practice in life to reduce your need for detoxification, choose whole foods over processed foods; consciously raised, well-treated local poultry, dairy, fish, and meats; and organic soy (tofu), fruit, and vegetables.

Tropical Fruits as Softening Agents

Tropical fruits with laxative or diuretic functions include tamarind and its juice, pineapple, wild custard apple, guava, pomegranate, coconut water (drink in moderation), banana, desert date, and figs.

— SP✷TLIGHT—

Pomegranate: From North Africa to Your Tummy, with Love

Contrary to popular belief, the pomegranate is not a fruit but the berry of an African and Asian tree *(Punica granatum).* The original Latin name for the tree, *Arbor punica,* means "Carthaginian tree," because Romans first encountered large groves of pomegranate trees growing in North Africa's famed city/state of Carthage ("Punic" refers to Carthage or its people). Rome waged war with Carthage in what were named the Punic Wars. Pomegranate's other names in Latin are *Malum punicum* (Carthaginian apple) and *Malum granatum* (seedy fruit). Pomegranate's popularity quickly spread, via the Romans, from ancient Carthage to the Mediterranean, Middle East, and parts of India.

Pomegranates have such a unique appearance that they have sparked many a myth and legend. The pomegranate has a long history in health and beauty and has been used as a medicine and nourishing food in Africa since at least the time of Egypt's New Kingdom (1570–1070 BC).

In holistic health, it is important not to isolate parts of the plant while disposing of the rest. Many parts of the pomegranate tree are useful, and knowing all of its uses rather than focusing solely on the berry can be helpful in your holistic health regimen.

> Pomegranate tree root bark is antihelmintic (destroys or causes expulsion of parasitic intestinal worms).
> The tree bark is also a vermifuge (expels worms).
> An astringent solution can be extracted from the root, bark, and berry rind (the rind is especially astringent).
> The dried pulverized rind is used to treat ulcers of the digestive tract.
> Pomegranate fruit is antidiarrheic (controls diarrhea) and hemostatic (arrests flow of blood or hemorrhaging).
> The ripe pomegranate berry is used to treat infections of the digestive tract.

Eat raw or juiced—these are the best way to consume the pomegranate berry, because of the high concentration of nutrients without the high content of sugar found in processed juice. Fresh pomegranate juice is a popular drink in the Middle East, especially with Persian (Iranian) and Indian cuisine. A hundred-milliliter serving of the juice provides 16 percent of the daily adult requirement of vitamin C. It is also a good source of pantothenic acid, potassium, and antioxidant polyphenols.

This chapter has presented a number of ideas from the herbal kingdom, inspired by the African diasporic practices for detoxification in a holistic sense. Cleansing of the nature covered in this chapter seeks to address the mind-body-spirit connection of any illness that presents itself. Many of the helpful African holistic detoxification practices are drawn from ancient Egypt (Khemet), though there are equally useful practices prominent to this day in the Caribbean that combine some Eastern elements.

CHAPTER 9

ELEMENTAL RITUAL: ANCIENT EGYPTIAN THERAPIES FOR THE SACRED AND MUNDANE

I t is generally believed that sub-Saharan Africans migrated from the ancient civilizations of Egypt. One place of particular importance to our conversation about holistic health is Khemet, for it is there that many traditions were established that continue to influence African American healing. This chapter explores elemental rituals—that is, rituals involving fire, water, air, earth, and akasha that originated in Egypt and ancient Khemet. The Khemetian use of saltwater in health ritual is stressed, as well as the beloved African diasporic practice of healing baths. This chapter gives you practical ways of imbuing your mind, body, and spirit with ancient healing from African recipes and rituals.

Hydrotherapy and Balneotherapy

Hydrotherapy is the therapeutic use of water in a bath, whirlpool, or natural body of water with submersion of a particular body part or the entire body. *Balneotherapy* is a manner of encouraging wellness and curing diseases, injuries, and other physical ailments through bathing or baths, utilizing natural springs, mineral waters, or the ocean.

When I sprained my ankle, my Aunt Edith offered the treatment of hydrotherapy combined with balneotherapy. She filled one stockpot with ice and a little water (way too little for my liking) and then another pot of just bearable-to-the-touch hot water. Back and forth she had me move my foot (pot to excruciating pot) until both pots of water were exactly the same lukewarm temperature and my swelling was beginning to subside. This was followed the next day by an Epsom salts soak, a type of balneotherapy.

— SP✴TLIGHT —

Salt

Salt is one of few known substances from ancient times used as a preservative. Egyptian mummies were preserved in a saltwater solution called natron or "birth fluid." Salt was accepted as a substitute in Egyptian burial rites for Mother's regenerative blood since it comes from the sea (womb).[1] Salts are believed to be rejuvenating to the overworked body, mind, and spirit.

Sea salt (sodium chloride) is the crystallized compound that comes from the ocean. A fine white salt comes from the Pacific Ocean. Salt is harvested from inland deposits left by ancient oceans in a mining process to yield table salt.

Sel gris (gray sea salt) comes coarse or fine. It contains clay from the salt marshes from which it is harvested. It is naturally high in magnesium and other minerals. It is slightly moist and processed mechanically.

Fleur de sel (flower of the salt) is a hand-raked gray salt rich in minerals. It is a gourmet salt, used for adding a finishing touch to a dish near the end of cooking to preserve its natural sweetness.

Himalayan pink salt is hand-mined from inside the Himalayan Mountains. The high-content mineral crystals, containing a hefty amount of eighty-four trace elements and iron, range in color from sheer white to varying shades of pinks to deep reds. This 250-million-year-old, Jurassic-era sea salt is used by gourmet chefs and holistic health professionals, spas, and others. These salts are promoted for their ability to stimulate circulation, lower blood pressure, and eliminate toxins such as heavy metals from the body. Lamps are also made from Himalayan pink salt. When lit, they emit negative ions, which are the beneficial ions concentrated at waterfalls, after a rainstorm, and at the ocean, among other natural sources. In addition to their refreshing, mood-lifting qualities, the negative ions emitted by the lamps purportedly help clear the air in the room in which they are lit of electronic pollution, the damaging positive ions emitted by electronic equipment and home appliances.

Epsom salts (magnesium sulfate) are added to bathwater to relax strained or bruised muscles. The combination of Epsom and Dead Sea salts in a bath can help the winter spirit reach a relaxed state.

Dead Sea salts have been renowned for their therapeutic benefits since ancient times because of their high mineral content:

Magnesium—combats stress and fluid retention as well as serving as an antioxidant.

Calcium—prevents water retention, increases circulation, and strengthens fingernails.

Potassium–energizes the body and balances skin moisture.

Bromides–ease muscle stiffness and relax the nervous system.

Sodium–is important for lymphatic fluid balance.

Benefits of Dead Sea salts have been proven in several clinical trials,[2] showing effectiveness as a treatment for patients with osteoarthritis, tendonitis, and psoriasis in as few as three to four baths a week, at a very low dilution (5 percent dilution for skin ailments and up to 10 percent dilution for osteoarthritis and tendonitis).

PAIN-RELIEVING SALT SOAK

3 cups Epsom salts

2 cups coarse Dead Sea salt

1 cup baking soda

1/2 cup sea kelp

1 teaspoon each: tamanu oil and lavender essential oil

Large glass or metal screwtop container

Combine first four ingredients in bowl. Sprinkle with essential oils. Stir. Pour into the container. Shake. Let rest 48 hours. Use two cups per bath. Soak for 20 minutes or more.

Tamanu *(Calophyllum inophyllum L.)*

You may be wondering why tamanu oil, also called foraha oil, is added to a bath soak. This rich oil, derived from the tamanu tree, indigenous to Southeast Asia, is filled with essential fatty acids and nutrients and is currently garnering attention as an oil of many cures. It has a lengthy folk history, with numerous traditional uses around the world. Examples of tamanu's many uses include:

> Soothes hemorrhoids.
> Tamanu sap combined with sulfur formulates an ointment for boils, open sores, and wounds.
> The Manus people of Papua New Guinea infuse its leaves over an open fire; once they are softened, the leaves are applied to a number of skin disorders, including boils, cuts, sores, ulcers, and acne or other skin breakouts.
> On Dobu Island, the leaves are decocted, and the resulting tea is used to cleanse skin rashes.
> Centuries ago, Jamaicans used tamanu to treat wounds and sores.
> Fijians use tamanu oil for joint pains, arthritis, bruises, oozing wounds, chapped lips, and diaper rash prevention.
> Pacific islanders apply it topically to scrapes, cuts, burns, insect bites and stings, acne and acne scars, psoriasis, diabetic sores, anal fissures, sunburn,

dry or scaly skin, blisters, eczema, diaper rash, and
herpes sores.

> The oil is used for several foot disorders, cracking
skin, and foot odor.

> Tamanu promotes new tissue formation,
accelerating healing and healthy skin growth.

> It is also a botanical used to treat muscle soreness
of many different types.

NOTE: Due to its pronounced medicinal aroma, try
using tamanu oil at night before bedtime or mask it with
pleasant-smelling, soothing essential oils like chamomile
or lavender.

GOOD SALT SOURCE

Salt Works, Inc.
15000 Wood-Red Rd NE, B-900
Woodinville, WA 98072
seasalt.com

Salt and the Goddess

By now it should be apparent that salt is a natural substance
used in bathing to encourage relaxation of muscles, reducing tension, body aches, and headaches. Salt is associated with spiritual
cleansing, nurturance, and the Mothers of the Sea (deities such
as Yemaya) as well. Thus it is also used ceremonially as a natural
amulet. Egyptian gods and goddesses play an important role in our
notion of salt as sacred, which may well be because of the mystical
quality of amniotic fluid.

The water jar is a symbol of the Egyptian goddess Nut. Nut is of the sky, sun, moon, and stars; she is also Mother to the Gods. Her essence pours down rain from the heavens filling the great seas. Nut is also the Milk-Giving Cow Goddess, Goddess of the Serpents of the Primeval Waters, Fertile Pig Goddess, Bird Goddess, and Goddess of the Underworld. Another water goddess, Isis, is the Great Mother Goddess of ancient Egypt. The universe and humanities sprung from her womb, nourished by her amniotic fluid.

As the essence of the great goddesses Nut and Isis, salt is the substance of purity, cleansing, luck, prosperity, compassion, love, hope, and renewal.

Herbal Baths: A Quimbois Healing Solution

Many different ADRs view the bath as a vessel of well-being. For example, in Quimbois, practiced by Africans in the French-speaking Caribbean, two main types of therapeutic baths are used:

1. *Bain demarre* (bath to rid of problems)
2. *Bain de la chance* (bath to bring good luck).

The baths are typically taken in plein air (outdoors). A big earthen pan filled with water is placed out in the sun. The Quimboiseur adds magickal herbs to the bath. Herbs used include paoca, calaba balsam *(Calophyllum calaba),* and bride's rose. In the heat of the warm Caribbean, sun tea steeps. Much like in Hoodoo, the fragrant waters are ladled ritualistically over the head nine times by the Quimboiseur, who also blesses the water with the appropriate spiritual intent through prayer and incantation.

Hoodoo's Healing Waters:
Antistress, Antianxiety, and Antidepressant

In the United States, the following formulas used by Hoodoos for rituals, for spiritual cleansing, in baths, and cosmetically feature aromatic waters or oil that address wellness in the body, mind, and spirit. It is interesting to note as well that these waters and washes bring together our folklore and appreciation for diverse cultural traditions.

Kananga Water: Ylang-ylang *(Cananga odorata)*, an herb that grows well in Asia, is an uplifting nervine and the main ingredient in Kananga Water, a ready-made product. The sweet, floral scent of ylang-ylang helps ease transitions by reducing anxious feelings, inhibitions, and stress. Kananga Water is a specific treatment for bereavement, separation, and longing, and may have applications for posttraumatic stress disorder (PTSD).

Chinese Wash: This wash contains broom straw, lemongrass *(Cymbopogon citratus, C. flexuosus)*, and citronella *(Cymbopogon nardus)* essential oil in a soapy solution. Chinese Wash spiritually and physically cleanses the home or business. Lemongrass has a pleasant, energizing, citrus aroma. Chinese Wash contains ingredients that were once primarily imported and then sold in the black community by Chinese merchants.

Florida Water: This water features some of the ingredients revered by ancient African empires, such as the Khemetian, in addition to herbs that continue to grow well in North Africa, Europe, and the United States. It contains bergamot *(Citrus bergamia)*, lavender *(Lavandula augustifolia)*, lemon *(Citrus limonum)*, jasmine *(Jasminum spp.)*, attar of roses *(Rosa spp.)*, and neroli bigarade *(Citrus aurantium)*. Florida Water is used for blessings, on altars, for spiritual cleansing, in baths, and as cologne. I personally love and highly recommend this special water.

Van Van: This is a preferred spiritual oil used as a perfume and in baths. It is made from African ingredients: lemongrass, vetiver *(Vetiveria zizanoides)*, castor oil, and jojoba oil with magnetic stones.

Gifts from the Elements

Let's now explore the nexus where hydrotherapy and balneotherapy connect up with the elements to produce a combined replenishment to the spirit and soul.

— SP☀TLIGHT —

Seaweeds

The sea is simultaneously calming and exhilarating. It is one of Earth's most spectacular natural features. Whether you're swimming, basking on the beach, or taking a brisk walk along the shore, being near the ocean will make you feel healthier, both mentally and physically. The same can be said about hair and skin-care products that contain one of the ocean's most important elements: seaweed. Sea vegetables contain ten to twenty times more minerals and vitamins than land vegetables.

I enjoy products that I formulate using sea kelp, a type of seaweed. After using bath products containing sea salts and seaweeds, I leave the tub feeling revitalized, tingly, and nourished.

There are many different types of seaweed. Following is a list of healthful, readily available types of seaweed you might find in hair products.

Kelp (Alaria esculenta): Kelps include wakame and kombu[3] *(Laminara japonica kombo)* and are sometimes called bladderwrack. Kelps contain alginic acid, which detoxifies by removing heavy metals, radioactive isotopes from the digestive tract and bones, as well as toxins from the hair. Evidence suggests that kombu may reduce estrogen; because lower estrogen levels provide less fuel for estrogen-dependent cancers like breast cancer, kombu is currently being investigated for the low breast cancer rate in postmenopausal Japanese women. Kombu also contains vitamins A, B complex, C, and E, part of the reason it nourishes the hair. Kelp is added to various foods like sushi and miso soup. It also is wonderful in hydrotherapy. I recommend the dried, cut, and sifted kelp as an additive for healing sea salt bath soaks and handmade soaps.

Dulse (Rhodymenia palmata): Dulse is a type of kelp similar to blackstrap molasses because it is very high in iron. It also is high in calcium, which is one of the most abundant mineral elements in the body, helping with strength and vitality.

Spirulina (Spirulina platensis): Spirulina is blue-green microalgae containing beta-carotene, an important antioxidant. Its green color is from chlorophyll. Dried, sifted spirulina is added to smoothies, soups, and teas by the level teaspoon and is used in some weight-sustaining and weight-loss formulas. In addition to its use in hair-care and skin-care products, spirulina is used to boost immunity to help fight diseases such as cancer, HIV/AIDS, and diabetes.

Consuming Seaweed

Consuming seaweeds helps health and beauty by improving overall vitality, encouraging healthy cell growth, and improving the hair's strength, shine, and growth. After all, when we are healthy on the inside, it shows on the outside. The following are some of the benefits of seaweed:

> When eaten regularly, may help combat some kinds of cancers, including cancer of the breast, ovaries, and uterus.

> Helps with feminine concerns such as mastitis when breastfeeding, irregular menstrual cycles, fibroids and ovarian cysts, infertility, PMS, and menopausal problems.

> Good source of calcium for the lactose intolerant.

> Helps regulate the thyroid, which in turn regulates the metabolism, conditioning the digestive system and helping reduce or maintain weight.

> Beneficial for pain, burns, and nervous conditions.

> Due to its emollient qualities, can be used as a hair and skin conditioner; defines and softens curls.

> Cultivates healthy skin and scalp due to its cell-renewing properties.

> As a trace mineral supplement, nourishing, rejuvenating, and aphrodisiac.

> Has antioxidant, antitoxic, antibacterial, and disinfectant properties.

HERBAL SEA SOAK

This recipe combines the healing properties of many different types of salt and seaweeds and an earthy evergreen scent created from a nurturing blend of essential oils.

2 cups Dead Sea salt

1 cup Himalayan pink salt

1/4 cup fleur de sel

1/4 cup sel gris

1/4 cup cut and sifted kelp

2 tablespoons pulverized dulse

2 tablespoons pulverized Iceland moss

1 tablespoon cut and sifted dried rosemary

1 tablespoon cut and sifted, pulverized dry lavender buds

10 drops Scottish pine essential oil

8 drops lavender essential oil

6 drops juniper essential oil

4 drops patchouli essential oil

Place salts, seaweeds, and dried herbs in a nonreactive bowl such as Pyrex or stainless steel. Stir to mix. In a separate small Pyrex bowl, combine essential oils, swirling to mix. Pour oils over salt-seaweed-herbal mixture. Stir with a stainless steel spoon. Place in a clean, dry glass jar with top. Shake gently each day for two to three weeks. Add one cup to bath. Makes enough for three baths; shelf life is three months if kept in a cool, dry location.

Cleansing with Smoke: Smudging

Smoldering resins and bark (incenses) and the ashes of specific plants are two ways of healing used in ancient Africa that continue in Africa and the diaspora. Khemetians used fragrant plants for the medicines and spiritual gifts they possess. Fumigation (smudging) with smoldering herbs was used during prayer, invocation, meditation, clearing, and healing. *Etu* is a term for burnt medicine, a healing way used in parts of West Africa. A well-known commercial example of *ashe*-rich etu medicine is "black soap."

There are probably healing trees right in your neighborhood or backyard, the barks and branches of which can be rolled tightly, bundled, and tied to create what we call a smudging wand or smudge stick. Loose incense, that is, incense made from finely ground barks, resins, rinds, and leaves, can be accentuated by the addition of the following tree medicines, revered by American healers of African descent and Black Indians as well.

Balsam fir *(Abies balsamae):* This sacred tree is used in blessing ceremonies. This fir has a pleasing, balsamic quality and is also considered cleansing and purifying.

Bearberry willow *(Salix uva-ursi):* This prominent healing tree is purging and purifying.

Cedar: Desert white cedar *(Juniperus monosperma)* and California incense cedar *(Calocedrus decurrens)* are the preferred smudging cedars. Cedar is burned during prayer, invocation, and house blessings. Cedar wards off illness in the home and in individuals. It works as a purifier and attraction herb when its wood chips are sprinkled over a hot charcoal block or smoldering mesquite.

Cedarwood *(Cedrus atlantica):* Wood chips of this tree can be used as a kindling source for other leaves and branches. Cedarwood is revered for its calming, balancing, ancient wisdom and is considered a protective plant that aids focus while bringing clarity. The physical aspects are perfect for spring smudging blends. It is antiseptic and energizing.

White cedar *(Thuja occidentalis):* This sacred tree, used primarily in spiritual ceremonies, is burned in purification rituals.

Juniper *(Juniperus communis):* The needles, berries, and wood of this revered tree are all useful in smudging blends. It is a celebrated tree for its uplifting, protective, purifying qualities, which boost confidence and energy levels. Juniper wards off illness and malicious intent.

Mesquite *(Prosopis glandulosa):* This fragrant wood is an ideal charcoal base for burning herbs during outdoor smudging.

Pine *(Pinus silvestris):* This tree is associated with endurance, perseverance, focus, trust, longevity, community, and stability. Healers celebrate the pine tree for its antimicrobial, antiseptic, tonic, stimulant, and restorative abilities. The healing medicine of the pine has been appreciated from ancient African civilizations to the present.

Pinon *(Pinus cembroides):* The needles of this pine are used in smudging rites, sometimes in place of sweetgrass.

Red willow (*Salix lasiandra):* Also called osier or Pacific willow, the red willow is prized by many and used in ceremonial healing.

White spruce *(Abies alba):* Considered a protective, renewing, grounding, and harmonizing tree, the white spruce enables us to regain focus and clarity. Other healing properties include antidepressant, antiseptic, and stimulant actions.

From the Ebers Papyrus

The Ebers Papyrus, from 1552 BC, which makes it the oldest pre-served medical document, lists more than eight hundred herbal remedies that combine water, fire, earth, or air with herbs and natural substances. You can tap into Khemetian healing in your own kitchen and bath or the great outdoors, as space permits. The following is a select group of aromatic herbs and other substances used in ancient Africa and the diaspora for ritual, ceremony, and body care.

Castor Oil (Ricinus communis)

Egyptians used castor oil in oil lamps, for headaches, and for skin and hair softening. African Americans and other African people use castor oil as an emollient lotion, hair growth aid, and laxative.

Clay

Mud baths are relaxing and help clear pimples that arise from hormonal fluctuations. There are purportedly numerous benefits of eating clay, an activity that Africans and African Americans have engaged in for centuries. Pure clay regulates the bowels, reduces headaches, and fights acne while also ridding the body of all sorts of toxins. Eating the refined pure clay, montmorillonite (referred to as bentonite), is recommended as a part of inner cleansing regimens. You may have heard of the Southern custom of clay eating. More properly called geophagy, from the Greek word *geophagia* (*geo*, form of *ge*, meaning "earth," and *phagein*, "to eat"), it is the custom of eating earthy or soil-like substances such as clay or earth.

Rhassoul mud (also called Ghassool): Africans and Africans in the Americas have a lengthy history of using clay for cleansing and nutrients. These days, there are numerous beauty products that contain Rhassoul, a mud that comes from the Atlas Mountains of Morocco. The mud is believed to be an excellent cleanser and detoxifier for the hair and skin. Covering yourself in mud sounds more like a way of getting dirty, but it really does cleanse, by drawing out impurities. Most mud formulas bring together the earth, air, and water element, which makes Rhassoul products an excellent way to encourage intimate contact with Nut and Isis.

Frankincense and Myrrh

As a tree-loving and in many ways tree-dependent culture, Khemetians had a great love for aromatic resins and fragrant herbs derived from all parts of the tree for holistic health purposes. Frankincense and myrrh are naturally occurring incenses sacred to the Khemetians. The two trees are kin as members of the Burseraceae family, which consists of about five hundred species divided into seventeen genera. Both of these resins are mildly sedative, though they can also be uplifting. The Khemetians used them in daily rites, funerary and mummification rituals, deity veneration, and celebration. Frankincense and myrrh offer a sacred invitation to Ra, Isis, Osiris, and Anubis. When the resins are used as essential oil, they take on the feminine form, suggestive of Isis. Since the attributes of Isis center on her protective abilities, she is thanked for security and abundance. Using frankincense and myrrh essential oils is important for the autumn and spring equinox and for winter solstice.

Frankincense is a tree often connected to high spirituality. It facilitates communication with various divine orders of beings including angelic spirits that carry our prayers and requests for protection to the highest spiritual realm. Frankincense is a heart purifier that encourages understanding and compassion, going so far as to heal the healer. It is burned to free the ill intent of nefarious spirits, purging their ill from the body and soul.

Myrrh is deep, dark, mysterious, and forceful. It is used for healing, strengthening, grounding, and purifying and for uplifting spirits, relieving mental and physical anguish, and releasing emotional blockages from the past.

Together, frankincense and myrrh are used the world over for helping humans in their desire to reach higher consciousness and commune with ascended masters. Serving as aromatic spiritual portals, frankincense and myrrh are capable of deepening spiritual connections, and thus are embraced by aromatherapists. The resins are important to holy celebrations and high holidays of various paths and faiths. This sacred Khemetian duo is useful for establishing consecrated space, speaking to the ancestors and spirits from the altar, and other specialized mind-spirit work.

Kyphi

This Egyptian healing substance is primarily used as incense, making it a strong representative of the fire element. Historically, kyphi was made from liquids, resins, fruit, spices, and herbs, such as red wine, honey, cassis, spikenard, saffron, mastic tree flowers, aspalathos, cinnamon, raisins, frankincense, and myrrh. Kyphi thrived in Egypt as both internal and aromatic medicine from the beginnings of the Old Kingdom through the last days of the New

Kingdom; after that, it could be found in Greece, Rome, and various African empires. Kyphi is used in prayer, invocation, meditation, divination, and dream work and to create a sacred space appealing to the gods and goddesses. Melding the elements with our akashic sensibility, kyphi engages us with the sacred. Renowned ancient Roman physicians Dioscorides and Galen recorded recipes. Today, a few manufacturers are working the ancient recipes' healing formulas, and the following are once again available.

Dioscorides' Kyphi: This type of kyphi was used in ancient Egyptian temples to Ra to welcome the evening. Dioscorides was a Greek-Turkish physician who lived from 40–90 CE. This kyphi recipe comes from his five-volume *De Materia Medica* on "the preparation, properties, and testing of drugs," which describes how plants were used medicinally in various cultures. The ingredients in this first-century kyphi include raisins, wine, and honey, as well as sweet flag, aspalathos, camel grass, and cyperus tubers. No fragrance oils or synthetics are added. The ingredients are mixed in a high-fired ceramic bowl with a wooden spatula to preserve their potency. Following the ancient Egyptian custom, ingredients are added one at a time to the base of chopped raisins resulting in very sweet incense that develops a spicy resinous quality. This type is a lighter blend, good for morning, afternoon, and dusk rituals.

Galen's Kyphi: This recipe comes from Galen (129–210 CE), a Greek physician and philosopher who studied in Egypt. This incense was used in ancient Egyptian temples to welcome the coming of night and was used medicinally to treat lung ailments and snake bites. Galen's Kyphi contains a specific portion of raisins, wine, honey, asphaltum, camel grass, sweet flag, cyperus tuber, saffron, spikenard, aspalathos, cardamom, and cassia. The blend yields a complex combination of lightly sweet and spicy resin with deep-earthy undertones. This subtle incense has a scent that is exceedingly relaxing, and is great for astral work. It is also recommended for rituals conducted at night.

Knowing and Sourcing Your Kyphi

An excellent and, in my experience, one of the few remaining authentic suppliers of various types of kyphi is: Alchemy Works, 643 Newtown St., Elmira, NY 14904; *alchemy-works.com*.

Lotus (Nelumbo nucifera, Nymphaea lotus)

Lotus plants were held in high esteem in ancient Egypt. *Nymphaea caerulea* is the species most frequently depicted in Egyptian art. For the Egyptians, the lotus was synonymous with love and became the focus for the mythic tales of creation, since it grows in water. The lotus was the primary accompaniment of women from the Old Kingdom until the decline of Egyptian civilization. Lotus oil was used in perfumery, for funerary rites as an unguent, and as an ointment for fever, as it was believed to have a cooling effect. The plant oil is slightly narcotic (causing sedation when larger amounts are used), bringing about deep relaxation and easing anxiety and inhibitions.

Pure lotus oil of the type favored by the Egyptians is extinct, but the lotus species currently available from the *Nymphaea* genus is lovely. The lotus oil we use now comes from white, pink, and blue flowers, each with a distinctive aroma.

> The white lotus, *Nymphaea lotus L.*, only blooms at night, a metaphor for sensuality and sexuality used by the Egyptians who thrived on such symbolism.

> Pink is rare, highly sought, and quite expensive; it may also be an acquired taste (I find it quite pungent).

> White and blue flower lotuses have a complex, earthy aroma kissed gently by the fragrance of fresh water.

Moringa (**Moringa stenopetala**)

Moringa oil comes from Egypt, the Sudan, and the Arabian Peninsula. It has a long history recorded in Egyptian medical papyri as a pregnant woman's belly rub, called *ben*. The oil is also used as lamp fuel and in soap, perfume, and skin care (as an emollient or softener).

Neroli

The exquisite and expensive pure neroli oil is derived from orange blossoms of *Citrus aurantium, C. brigaradia,* and *C. vulgaris.* Neroli is a potent scent; used in perfumery, its fragrance is precious, unusual, sweet, floral, penetrating, and alluring. Orange blossom is used to deter dermatitis, to quell stomach upset, for menstrual and menopausal discomforts, and to fight infection. Neroli essential oil and orange blossom water are thought to have antidepressant, antianxiety, and antihysteria effects and are used to ease inhibitions and elevate self-esteem.

WARNING: Neroli is a heart tonic and those with heart disease must use it only under the supervision of an herbalist or naturopathic doctor.

Orange (Citrus sinesis)

We are most familiar with oranges as the juicy fruit consumed during our daily morning rituals. As a symbol of Sun Ra, the orange plant is one of nature's most invigorating gifts, rich in its potential for healing. Many parts of the orange tree are used for holistic healing and in complementary therapies. One of the most intoxicating parts, however, is the blossoms (see Neroli).

Rose (Rosa spp.)

In the distant past, roses were revered for their medicinal and culinary applications (as well as their inviting aroma), rather than their appearance, as they are in more modern times. Roses are associated with the Queen of Sheba, Nefertiti, and Cleopatra. Thankfully, herbalists are once again leading the public to understand that the rose is not just a pretty flower but also a potent healer. Roses have been used since ancient times as a nervine, systemic tonic, refrigerant, and aphrodisiac. African Americans (among others) burn dried petals by themselves or in an incense blend to attract good luck; they also use rose petals, rose essential oil, or attar of roses in baths. Attar of roses is the pure rose oil derived from the Bulgarian damask rose *(Rosa damascena)*.

WARNING: Some practitioners suggest complete avoidance of concentrated rose products during pregnancy; they stimulate the womb. If you are pregnant, consult your natural practitioner before using rose products.

Khemetian and Yoruba Sacred Baths

This segment draws clear correlations between Khemetian use of scent and specialized baths to communicate with deities and use in the Yoruba path of Ifa.

In the *Metu Neter Vol. 1*, by Ra Un Nefer Amen, a direct relationship is established between the Yoruba traditional practice called Ifa and Khemetic (Egyptian) spirituality. For example, Ra Un Nefer connects Ifa Orishas and Khemetian deities with the same attributes. Each deity discussed has associated spiritual baths, incenses, and herbal medicines both to pay spiritual homage and for healing. In Ifa, each Orisha has a corresponding herb called *ewe* in the Yoruba language. This unique application of aromatic healing is not limited to the Yoruban-based Ifa faith; it is prevalent in most African diasporic practices. Here are a few examples of the Khemetic and Ifa continuum.[4] Baths bring devotees into the realm of each deity, as do oils. Incense is used for invocation and prayer.

Shango (Ifa) and Heru (Khemetic) are gods of action and will.

> Baths: geranium, bay leaf
>
> Oils: olibanum (frankincense) and geranium
>
> Incense: olibanum[5]

Shango is also associated with cayenne, sarsaparilla, cedar, and lightning.[6]

Oshun (Ifa) and Het-Heru (Khemetic) are goddesses of life and sexuality.

> Baths: yellow roses, honeysuckle, vetiver, spearmint, sandalwood
>
> Oils: rose, sandalwood, honeysuckle, and cinnamon[7]

Oshun is associated with lotus, chamomile, and myrrh.[8]

Elegba (Ifa) and Sebek (Khemetic) are gods of wisdom and divinity; human and godly.

> Baths: lavender, oregano, larkspur
>
> Oils and incense: lavender and lily of the valley[9,10]

Yemaya (Ifa) and Auset (Khemetic) are goddesses of humanities, creation, and nurturing.

> Baths: spearmint
>
> Oils and incense: jasmine, spearmint[11,12]

Ogun (Ifa) and Herukhuti (Khemetic) are gods of war, justice, and metal.

> Bath: pine
>
> Oils: pine, cedarwood
>
> Incense: pine, tobacco, and cedarwood.

Ogun is associated with eucalyptus.[13,14]

Khemetian Elemental Cleansing

The Khemetian way of cleansing goes beyond soap and water by utilizing water, air, fire, akashic energy, earth, and salts. You can incorporate some of the Khemetian approach to elemental hydrotherapy to mark the solstices, equinox, or other special days.

Water

> > Liberally use natural salts in the bath (up to two cups per bath).
> > Drink herbal teas with astringent, diuretic, or laxative properties to cleanse the colon and flush the kidneys: uva-ursi sacred bark, senna, dandelion roots, flaxseed, or calendula. Cleansing and detoxification of this sort should be done under supervision of a health professional; excessive use can be harmful.

> Use clay or Rhassoul mud to pull impurities out through the skin, our largest organ. Certain types of clay can also be taken internally to bind and then remove impurity from our systems.

Fire and Akasha
> Use the heavenly natural fruit and resin incense called kyphi or a combination of frankincense and myrrh.

Fire, Earth, Air
> Bring aromatic herbs and candles into the bath.

Air, Water, Earth
> Add scented waters as well as flower petals and oils to your bath.

Water, Earth, Air, and Fire
> Focus on the sensual: scented candles, the aroma of smoldering kyphi, floral waters and essential oils (frankincense, myrrh, rose, neroli, or lotus) sprinkled in the bath (8–10 drops per full bath) to get you through the trials of fasting.

Nefertiti's Milk Bath and Ritual

Queen of Egypt, Nefertiti was acclaimed for luminous beauty that radiated from the inside. She was an active leader and vibrant companion to King Amenhotep III. The two had a unique vision, previously unheard of in Egypt: They wanted their kingdom to worship one almighty god, Aten the sun god. They designed the capital city of Amarna to shine with spirituality and the arts. Queen Nefertiti was a wisewoman we can continue to contemplate when overwhelmed by life.

Ritual Preparations

1. Play authentic Egyptian music; try *Fire Dance, Music of the Nile,* or *Drummers of the Nile* ("Halawa Ya" track).

2. Place salt pyramids for purification and protection in the cardinal directions of bathroom. (Mix a cup each coarse sea salt, fine sea salt, and Dead Sea or Himalayan salt, and then create the mounds.)

3. Place lotus, neroli, and rose candles on a brass plate or glass with golden rim (symbolic of Sun Ra). Surround the candles with river rocks, representing the River Nile.

4. Set an Isis and Osiris statue with an ankh amulet on the edge of bathtub or nearby, if desired as a focal point for reflection.

NEFERTITI'S MILK BATH RECIPE

In North Africa, queens of Nefertiti's day often took milk baths combined with fragrant and healing herbs as a balm for their sun-parched skin. Nefertiti's Milk Bath is useful during transitions of the seasons or life passages.

1 cup whole milk or cream

1 cup orange blossom water

1/4 cup aloe vera gel

1/8 teaspoon each: attar of rose and myrrh and
    frankincense essential oils

1/2 cup Rhassoul mud

1 cup rose petals

Plug the tub. Run water in and add milk. Put orange blossom water in a bowl and whisk in aloe vera gel, followed by
attar of rose, myrrh, frankincense, and Rhassoul mud. Pour
the mixture into the bath, under the running tap. Once the
tub is half full, turn off the water and add the rose petals.
Set fragrant candles (lotus, rose, and orange) on a fireproof
plate; surround the candles with river rocks symbolic of the
Nile. Light the candles and place near the tub.

Once in the bath, sit back and relax; soak in the sensual
collage of sound, scent, fire, earth, ancient memory, and
nurturing water. Take deep cleansing breaths. Exhale
anxiety. Focus on the flickering flames of the candles and
statuary to transport your soul to a different space and time.

Smooth moringa oil lightly scented with a few drops of neroli or rose oil on wet body while still in the bath; treat rough
areas (heels, elbows, bottoms of feet, hands) with castor
oil. Dab lotus oil on chakras. Continue to relax and enjoy the
candles and music until you are fully satiated. This is a very
sensual treat, deserving partnership to heighten its full tan-
tric (sensual spirituality rather than purely sexual) potential.

Elemental Khemetian Healing of Past and Present

The Khemetian practices and ingredients explored in this chapter bring ancient Egypt alive and allow us to see the vibrant healing
continuum they represent. The ancient concept of healing through
water, salts, earth, fire, and air was passed down to us, bringing a

powerful synergistic healing *(ashe)* provided by a fusion of the elements. This healing modality has been embraced and transformed in contemporary ADRs like Quimbois, Hoodoo, and Vodou.

The attempt to harness the collaborative forces of nature, so vital to West African healing, in which it is refered to as *ashe* and in some cases *nyama*, stimulates our akashic self. This in turn helps our mind and spirits ascend, elevating us to new capacities for compassion and healing. We open like petals of the lotus, awakened through Earth Mother's gifts, observing previously hidden dimensions, revealing doors to fresh possibilities holding treasure chests of wellness. This New World approach to age-old healing paradigms goes far beyond the limitations of Western culture's focus on the physical body in illness. Healing through each of the elements in mind, body, and spirit may be one of the greatest yet still underutilized gifts of Khemetian wellness.

CHAPTER 10

TRIBAL BEAUTY: ANCIENT EGYPTIAN BEAUTIFICATION FROM THE SOUL OUTWARD

ribal beauty radiates from the inside of the soul, through the crown, and back down to the soles of the feet. Preferred spiritual colors that enhance beauty according to the Yoruba medicinal concept include: black (dudu in Yoruba), which is like the color of our skin and symbolic of wise containment; red (pupa), which is representative of healthy blood underneath the skin that brings an omnipresent glow; and white or colorless fluids (funfun) such as kaolin clay, used for contact and mediation with the spiritual realm, an important space for cultivating and maintaining inner calm that presents itself as beauty.

Tribal beauty is built around luminosity, which is enhanced by certain tree medicines, body butters, natural oils, and phytonutrients consumed, inhaled, or applied. In this chapter, we look at the many ways and specific methods by which tribal beauty may be achieved.

The Songhai Way to Healthy Beauty

We begin our journey through African tribal beauty by looking first at the ancient Songhai Empire, a precolonial West African empire. Like many other African cultures, the Songhai world is populated by numerous spirits that live in all aspects of the natural world, who are said to come together for the good of humankind. As such, the Songhai believe that certain illnesses and disorders can be cured by combining wildcrafted and harvested flowers, herbs, roots, and stems of the forest and savanna with domesticated products from farms such as milk, cheese, yogurt, eggs, grains, vegetables, and fruits. The advantage of each type of energy enhances that of the others. The synthesis is an unusually strong beauty medicine.

The Songhai philosophy is actualized through a combination of cultivated dairy products and wildcrafted, harvested natural ingredients. Dairy products are nutritious, reinforcing, emollient, and softening, and they especially have these properties when paired with fruits, vegetables, herbs, and nut oils. Drink a Songhai Smoothie or a Veggie Milk to engage in these principles.

SONGHAI SMOOTHIE

This multipurpose smoothie is fragrant, soothing, moisturizing, rich, and tasty. Designed for parched skin, it also embodies the Songhai philosophy of blending the elements of nature. The Songhai Smoothie contains vitamin-rich strawberries and alpha-hydroxy–imbued buttermilk to nurture sensitive skin. The emollience of peach flesh, peach kernel oil, and creamy coconut milk, balanced with soothing chamomile and oat straw, makes this the perfect skin concoction. The only problem with this treat is deciding between drinking it or applying it to the face and body. (I suggest a bit of both.)

1/3 cup strawberries

1 small, ripe peach

1/2 cup coconut milk

1 1/2 cups buttermilk

1 bag chamomile tea

1 tablespoon oat straw

Wash, peel, and finely chop strawberries and peach (use organic). Crush the peach pit with a mortar and pestle or mallet. Add these ingredients to Pyrex baking dish. Pour milks over fruit, add herbs (leaving tea in bag), and stir. Cover and infuse mixture in an oven set at 170° F for two hours. Remove from oven; whisk mixture. Pour through a fine sieve. Use cheesecloth to remove peach kernel and tea bag, then firmly press remaining mixture using the back of a large spoon to extract juices and herbal medicine. Whisk again and repeat the straining and squeezing process. Dab on to face and neck, leave on for five minutes, and rinse well with cool water. There is no need for furthering this treatment with lotions or creams because it will leave your face soft and moist. You can pour this in your bath for a luxurious moisturizing soak, or sip it through the day, as it is tasty, nutritious, and relaxing to the nerves. Makes 16 ounces; use within three days.

Alpha Hydroxy Acids

Alpha hydroxy acids (AHAs) are a class of chemical compounds that are made of carboxylic acid. They are naturally occurring or synthetic and are often used in the cosmetics industry. In natural cosmetics, they are used to reduce visible signs of aging while conditioning the hair and skin. AHAs include glycolic acids from sugar cane, lactic acids derived from dairy products, citric acids derived from citrus fruits, malic acids from apples and pears, and tartaric acid from grapes.

Tip: Want to be extra gentle and knowledgeable about what you put onto your delicate face and eye area while being economical at the same time? Make your own cosmetics! A very good source for making your own AHA-based masks is *www.makeyourowncosmetics.org*.

VEGGIE MILK

The Songhai-inspired combination of ingredients in Veggie Milk helps alleviate many skin disorders. The bleaching action of the buttermilk makes it especially helpful for those with freckles, scars, uneven skin tones, and skin discolorations. AHA-rich buttermilk also gently removes dry skin so you won't look ashy in dry and cold weather. Buttermilk encourages cell renewal, which slows the appearance of wrinkles and tightens saggy skin. The lipids in buttermilk are emollient, so they keep your face moist but not greasy. Cucumbers are an astringent, helping to alleviate shiny noses and foreheads. Lettuce is excellent for cleansing skin prone to acne. Carrots contain healthy doses of vitamins A and E, which help check the onset of wrinkles while bringing a youthful glow to the skin. Both buttermilk and carrots make Veggie Milk safe for oily and combination skin. Use organic vegetables if possible.

2 carrots

1 cup iceberg lettuce

1/2 cup cucumber

2 cups buttermilk

Set oven at 170° F. Scrub carrots and cucumber. Rinse them and the lettuce. Spin vegetables in a salad spinner. Peel carrots and cucumber. Cut the cucumber in half lengthwise and scoop out seeds. Shred lettuce, carrots, and cucumber in a food processor with shredder attachment or with a hand grater. Put the vegetables in an ovenproof bowl or small baking pan made of Pyrex and cover with buttermilk. Place in the oven and cook for two hours, stirring occasionally. Drain through sieve placed over a large bowl. Pour veggie milk into a sterilized bottle. To use, pour a small amount of the milk onto a cotton swab and dampen face and neck gently. Leave on for three to five minutes. Rinse thoroughly with cool water; pat lightly with towel to dry. Use instead of soap in the morning and before bedtime. Makes approximately 12 ounces; shelf life is one week, refrigerated.

Luminous Blackness

Whereas shiny hair is one of the most celebrated features for just about every other culture, vibrant, glowing, or red-toned[1] *skin* is a distinctly African quality, noted in our figurative sculptures, and it is a concept of beauty that has survived and thrives to the present day. We are very concerned with the quality of our skin. We wonder: Is my skin too shiny, dull, blotchy, and uneven? African descended people across the diaspora frown upon "ashy" (dried or white in appearance) skin. We seek balanced skin, radiant and luminous—a fitting window to the depth of blackness.

In considering the Songhai way to health and beauty, try the following additional, super-simple ways of bringing luminosity and clarity to your skin.

Buttermilk Mask

Buttermilk was once a mainstay in the African American diet and is still used in many of our soul food recipes (e.g., fried chicken, biscuits and gravy, fish). This recipe brings the Songhai beauty way together with this beloved African American healthful ingredient.

Pour one half cup buttermilk in a bowl. Wash and pat face and hands dry. Apply buttermilk mask to face with cotton ball. Lie back so mixture doesn't drip off. Remain reclining 20 minutes. Rinse and dry. This will leave your skin emollient, and with consistent use, reduces signs of visible aging. For a *Yogurt Facial,* do the buttermilk mask, but use full-fat yogurt instead of buttermilk. Yogurt will bring all the same benefits as buttermilk.

Egg White Mask

Again harkening back to the Songhai use of dairy in their health preparations, here is a mask designed to tighten and refine your face and neck. Wash your face and hands, pat dry. Break open two organic, vegetarian-fed, free-range eggs, separating the white from yolks. Whisk the egg whites till frothy. Lie back. Apply egg whites to your face. Let dry completely until a tight mask forms. Let sit and tighten for ten minutes. Rinse thoroughly with cool water.

Shea Butter Care

Shea butter is grown in various parts of Africa and processed by hand in a laborious process by African women and children. Shea butter is extremely popular in the black community on both sides of the Atlantic. It will add a beautiful glow to your skin and hair. Just melt some in the palm of your hand using natural body heat, and apply where desired. Shea butter has the additional benefits of protecting the skin from UV rays, deterring sunburn and sun damage, and having a long shelf life.

African Sausage Tree Oil

The sausage tree *(Kigelia pinnata)*, or *kigeli-keia* as it is called in Mozambican Bantu, is a tropical species that grows in the eastern part of South Africa (such as Swaziland), Namibia, Mozambique, Zimbabwe, and northward as far as Tanzania. It grows on river banks or close to rivers and large streams elsewhere in tropical Africa, from Eritrea to Chad and west to Senegal.

The sausage-shaped fruit of this tree grows up to fifty centimeters in length and ten in diameter. The fruit is a dull greenish-gray to pale brown, hard, and very heavy. It hangs from a very long, sturdy stalk. The fruit falls in March and April, which can be a dangerous time of the year to be near the trees if you are unaware—ouch! Fruit remains undamaged on the ground for many months after falling.

This fruit produces an extraordinary oil, which has been shown to even the skin tone, protect the skin from UV rays, repair sun damage, and even help fight skin cancer (melanoma). Buy some and apply neatly to your face and body before spending time outdoors and then again upon your return indoors.

South African people, Khoi and San, as well as my ancestors the Tsonga and other Bantu-speakers, have a long history of using sausage tree oil to fight, treat, soothe, and attract or deter specific conditions. For example, it is used to combat:

> Fungal infections

> Skin ailments such as eczema, psoriasis, boils

> Serious skin ailments such as leprosy

> Ringworm, tapeworm

> Postpartum hemorrhaging

> Diabetes

> Pneumonia

> Toothache

> Piles (use boiled roots, stem, and bark)

> Gonorrhea (use a decoction of bark)

> Rheumatism (use as a wash)

Tsonga women also use sausage tree oil as a cosmetic against the sun and for its antiaging properties, and it is sometimes even used as an aphrodisiac.

The seed oil, pulp, bark, roots, rind, and an extract of the fruit are all used medicinally in the following ways:

> Sausage tree fruit extract is being researched as a skin cancer treatment.

> The fruit extract is used in cosmetics to even complexion.

> Sausage tree fruit extract is added to numerous "breast firming" formulas.

> The fruit extract is used for wrinkle reduction.

> Fruit extract of sausage tree contains antioxidants good for stimulating hair growth and maintaining the natural condition of kinky, curly, and wavy hair.

> It is an effective burn treatment.

> Sausage tree fruit extract helps with pimples, razor burn, and other rashes.

> The fruit extract is used against skin infections.

Coconut

Coconut has its mad fans and ardent detractors—some love it and others despise it. I know well, as a member of the hand-soap maker's community, that it is said to be drying to the skin, particularly if used as a large part of a soap base. Coconut soaps are very useful for cleansing oily skin, as they make a frothy cleansing lather. The ability of coconut soaps to form a thick lather, even in saltwater, have made coconut oil soaps popular with seafaring people for centuries. Coconut oil can be combined with cocoa butter or shea butter to create a balanced soap that is neither too astringent nor excessively emollient. For those who find certain African body butters, which contain emollients that might overwhelm normal or combination skin, too thick or too oily, coconut is your better alternative. Coconut cream or another coconut product can serve as a light moisturizer.

Coconut Crème

Coconut crème is gaining popularity as a botanical for skin and hair care—but not the type in cans in the food aisle! Coconut crème is a cosmetic cream available from Togo, where women and children villagers hand-press the coconuts to extract creamy oil. This virgin coconut oil is pressed from fresh coconut milk and meat rather than the copra (dried meat or dried kernel). Coconut crème works well as massage therapy oil because of its silky texture. In parts of Africa, such as Togo, coconut crème has been used traditionally as a hair conditioner, strengthener, and growth aid. Coconut crème or oil can be applied to the skin and hair before swimming to protect it from damage, lending a lovely scent as well.

To Use: Rub the oil into the scalp and hair ends (for brittle, split ends) or try this hot oil treatment. Melt oil, cool slightly, and then apply to the scalp and ends using a boar-bristle paintbrush. Follow with a gentle shampoo. This approach is preferable for those with an oily scalp.

The Edible Oil: Cocoa Butter

Cocoa butter is an African body butter that contains no solvents; it is a human food-grade ingredient. The edible aspect is appealing to those who desire wholesome, nurturing ingredients in homemade potions, creams, and healing balms. Most chocolate also contains cocoa butter as well as shea butter; though you may not have thought of eating cocoa butter, you most likely already have. Cocoa beans are useful, productive, and popular because they are 15 percent fat. The oil is very attractive as an ingredient in herbal cosmetics—cheap, readily available, and multipurpose, with a very long shelf life. Cocoa butter is highly popular in the African American community and has been for a very long time. In Africa, it was traditionally used as a skin softener, emollient, pregnant and postpartum belly rub, stretch mark healer, and soothing substance for burns.

Kalahari Seed Oil

As discussed earlier in the book, Kalahari seed oil is derived from watermelon seeds, one of our favorite soul foods. This uniquely powerful seed oil reduces the visible signs of aging because of its potent antioxidants. It is also useful on the hair and skin as a conditioner and gentle emollient. Kalahari seed oil provides protection from damaging UV rays—protecting the hair and skin from being ravaged by sun and wind. It is used as a pre-shampoo hot oil treatment or applied directly to hair, scalp, and skin, and is added to numerous prepared hair and skin-care products.

Camwood: The Inner Dimension

To add a metaphysical dimension to skin care, camwood is still tops. Camwood *(Baphia nitida),* also known as African sandalwood, has strong *pupa* (red) colorant strength, symbolic of safety and concealment, two significant features of Yoruban medicine that have carried over to New World secret doctoring.[2] Without a doubt, we like red and seek a reddish-sunny glow to our complexion.

Red Skin Medicine #1

When ground and made into a paste, camwood is left on black skin, as well as on braided or tightly curled or cropped hair—spiritual makeup, if you will, that leaves the wearer with a red-coated, otherworldly, and provocative appearance.

Red Skin Medicine #2

Red palm oil is used in African massage to improve circulation and raise the skin color as well. Red palm oil, like camwood, has an immense spiritual dimension important to African wellness philosophy.

White-Faced with Spiritual Kaolin

Red is important because it shows good quality of blood and, in turn, this indicates good health as reflected in the complexion. Black is important because it walks the careful balance of what is hidden and what is revealed; it offers simultaneously a cloak and glass through which to comprehend wellness. There is another important color in the trilogy: white. As I mentioned, white means *funfun* (in Yoruba, white or clear color) and is associated with the spirit realm and spirits generally. White is our cells, sperm, saliva, rain, water, tears, the body's internal essence.

Many African masks and figures, including the exquisite Baule idealized figures, typically feature recessed eyes accentuated with kaolin. In life, Baule seers, as well as others in many parts of sub-Saharan Africa, apply kaolin (pure white clay) to their eyes and lips. Being the color of the spirits, it enables its wearers to see and hear the spirits more clearly and vice versa.

Kaolin not only facilitates communication with the spirit world, it is a holistic medicine that cleanses and purifies the body. When taken internally, kaolin works by pulling and then binding toxins from within, allowing your body to purge them as waste through bowel movements.

Mende and Sherbro Notions of Beauty

We can learn a great deal about cultural iconic beauty through the art and artifacts of various tribes.

The Mande people have a beautiful, black *Theng* mask that acquires its desired darkened hue by being rubbed multiple times with palm oil. *Teli,* or blackness and wetness, refers to the origins of

Mande knowledge—dark, deep, and contained. It also refers to the nature spirits who live in the river, embodying the medicine found within. During masquerade, girls initiated into the local secret society have their dark skin oiled to represent the underwater spirits. When performed at night, this ceremonial production takes on an eerie, otherworldly quality, reinforced by the depth and mystery of blackness.

The Sherbro, a culture living near the Mende, associate holistic cures, especially of mental conditions, and agricultural fertility with a potent medicine or spiritual force. The current-day Sherbro Island is in Sierra Leone, and the land of Sherbro includes the Kanwo and Sitwa chiefdoms.

At the core of Sherbro societies are women. Behku Mama is the supreme head, followed by Yamama and Kambeh. Each of these women is a high-ranking official looking out for the better good of her community.

Rather than looking toward youth as the main source of beauty, Sherbro ideals of cultivated refinement include wholesome, mature womanhood. These women have sophisticatedly styled hair; the styling skill comes with age and practice. It is typically corn-rowed or braided, sometimes accentuated with a glamorous headband, with luminous black skin and a long neck enhanced by pronounced neck rings.

The Mende have a similar society to the Sherbro, called *Njayie*. Both Sherbro and Mende female initiation societies feature a full-bodied female figurine as their representative that stands beside the medicine at the special meetinghouse. These works of art feature a similar idealized female aesthetic, demonstrating the powerful connection between transcendent beauty and the ability to mediate with the spiritual world.

Transcendent Beauty: The Baule of Côte d'Ivoire

The Baule people of Côte d'Ivoire make outstanding representations of humans that show another type of idealized, transcendent beauty. Typically, the torsos of these figures are marked by three small raised points across the chest and a vertical column of points topped by several diagonal stripes. Once called scarification, it is now more appropriately called "citification," which deletes the negative connotations of the word "scar." Of course, the hair is outstanding and noticeable—typically arranged in an elaborate braided or twisted coiffure with patterned bands pulled back in parallel rows. Ornamentation includes delicate strands of natural seed beads around the neck and hips and below that, metal bands, and then more strands of seed beads about the feet.

You can tell beauty when you see it in a Baule figure. The posture is upright and proud; the citification marks show care, attention, and sometimes tribal identification; the ornaments are subtle yet evidently carefully selected and, of course, there is the vigilantly coiffed hair. You can tell from gazing upon these figures that the manner in which the body is adorned is important. The faces are kept well intact so that they can connect with the gaze of humans and the attention of spiritual entities. Blood offerings are made toward the feet, never at the face, keeping the beauty restored and renewed from the sole level.

Posture

Posture is important as an indication of wellness, respect, bearing, and character. For example, in an idealized Guro figure from Côte d'Ivoire, the eyes are narrowed, which adds mystery not found in the direct gaze. The arms are typically relaxed, to show an even and cool nature. Legs are similarly poised. Slightly outstretched arms offer a positively embracing action. The exposed breasts of a woman communicate un-fathomable power. A woman thus poised, relaxed yet defiant, suggests, "I can give you life or make your life a living hell." Rather than a source of scandal, shame, or Freudian sexualizing, the traditional African topless female is an emblem of communal power.

Natural Adornment

Take inspiration from our Sudanese, Berber, and Taureg brothers and sisters. Wear flowing, all natural, breathable fabric (such as cotton or hemp)—long-sleeved, fairly well fitted, light colored or white robes. White attracts energy of a pure, cleansing nature, and it also reflects the sun, so it is cooling. Weather permitting, I will add a natural wool, cotton, or silk shawl to keep desired energy hidden and inside, while opening the shawl to release that which is not. The Taureg of North Africa's Morocco and environs use turbans as well to conceal their thoughts and protect their identity.

Leaning toward sustainable fibers such as bamboo, organic cotton, hemp, and recycled substances accentuates luminous beauty by helping Mother Earth sustain her resources—keeping the planet and ourselves beautiful at once. Natural accents complete the beauty.

> Flowers, such as the fragrant gardenia worn by Billie Holiday, bring out the natural beauty of the tribal woman as well as add a hypnotic scent.

> Shells, particularly cowry shells, are a beloved emblem of beauty and mysterious feminine power as well as prestige, frequently worn by men and women of African descent.

> Seed beads come in many different shapes, sizes, and colors. Taking the lead from African figurative sculpture, we can achieve a natural type of beauty by decorating the wrists, ankles, neck, and waist with strung beads. Stringing beads is also a relaxing and meditative activity, so there is an added bonus to making them yourself.

— SP☀TLIGHT—

Cotton *(Gossypium spp.)*

Cotton is one of the most important economic botanical plants in the world. It was a major impetus for the need of an ample, unpaid labor force that inspired slavery in the American south. Even the story of how the plant migrated is full of intrigue and controversy. My favorite is the story of how it probably became a stowaway in some long-ago vessel that was making its way to the New World.

Cotton and Africans came together in a brutal way, under the poorest possible conditions. Still, enslaved Africans carried out the orders of their owners, planting, picking, and helping to process more cotton than thought humanly possible. African women, who were charged with a great deal of the health care on the plantation for both blacks and whites, and particularly as midwives for women's health, soon discovered cotton root's abortifacient qualities. This discovery enabled midwives to induce labor for already deceased (stillborn) fetuses. Cotton root decoction also allowed the women who endured rape by planters and their associates, as well as the prospect of having their offspring sold away into slavery, the ability to terminate unwanted pregnancies. Please note, before you get any ideas, this is a very dangerous activity (abortifacient herbalism). I am not suggesting that anyone self-treat using cotton root bark, because the results could be lethal!

Cotton is a biennial or triennial herb with a round branching stem about five feet high. It has a hairy palm-shaped leaf and yellow flowers. The fruit (the boll is considered a fruit because it contains seeds) is a three-to-five-inch celled capsule in which seeds are held. An Asian native, cotton is cultivated throughout the world. The U.S. Pharmacopeia (USP) recognized cotton in 1863 and 1916 for its effects on the uterine organs. In the nineteenth century, the active constituent was named "gossypiin," an obvious link to its botanical name.

Historically, the inner bark of the young root was used as an abortifacient. This use among enslaved African Americans was reported as early as 1840. In Euro-American medicine, the bark of the root was used in cases of difficult labor, uterine inflammation, sterility, vaginitis, and suppressed menstruation.[3]

Today we use cotton as a styptic, to hold medication to wounds, and to cover fresh wounds so they can still breath; to hold poultice, infusion, decoction, vapors, and rubs; to cleanse the face and apply makeup or sacred ornamentation; to secure henna tattoo to allow the stain to seep into the upper layer of the skin; to clean and cover the ears and blow the nose; and, of course, for clothing. Organic, naturally dyed cottons are a wholesome option available today that are less likely to irritate delicate skin and are kinder to the environment than cotton processed commercially. Organic, naturally dyed cotton is expensive. To cut costs, seek organic cotton garments or bedding in resale shops, on *eBay.com,* or as bulk fabric to design and sew your own apparel.

Spiritual Feeling Close to the Vest: Wearing Green Clothing

Recently, Bono of the Irish rock group U2 and also an activist, has turned to clothing design, along with his wife, Ali Hewson. The two are working in collaboration with the designer Rogan to have clothes made by the people of Lesotho in Southern Africa and Tunisia in northern Africa. The clothes are chic with a combination of art nouveau, Renaissance, and East Indian flair. The line was created to support fair-trade practices and sustainable income for impoverished communities while shunning the notion of children working in sweatshops. The clothing line is called Edun ("nude" backward). Edun features organic hemp and cotton, the poetry of Rilke, and whimsical embellishments. The Edun line is mentioned because of its emphasis on developing equitable trade schemes in villages where people of the Motherland live.

There are similar fair-trade projects involving economic crops all around the world. Today, it is possible to truly dress in a spiritual manner, knowing the clothes on your back benefit a developing country (as well as the global environment) in a sustainable way. Keep your eyes peeled for organic clothing created with healing spirit in your community. In the virtual community there is an extensive listing of eco-friendly, fair-trade, and sustainable clothing lines, that also happen to be fashionable, for men, women, and children.

Find Out More . . .

For more "green" clothing options, check out *treehugger.com*, including the article "Queer Eye for the Green Guy" (March 15, 2005) in the archives.

Royal Crown

In African society, the crown is really the glorified point on the human form. In Africa and the New World, all sorts of ornamentation and accentuation is used to bring out the beauty of the head.

> Heads are shaved or close-cropped to show beautiful head shapes.

> A colorful headband is used to bring color into the hair near the face and to bring shape and enhanced beauty to the hairstyle.

> During worship, the crown is adorned with delicate feathery hats, fabric and lace hats, and symbolically white millinery to indicate high position.

> Whether in or out of style, head-wrapping remains a mainstay in black culture. Head wraps are used to accentuate beauty,

framing the face with lovely patterns, shapes, and colors. The coverings are used for religious, spiritual, and style reasons. In the United States, we call them head ties, head handkerchiefs, tignons, turbans, and head coverings.

Saying No to Yivi Yivi

Yivi yivi is a Mande term to describe the display of messy hair. *Yivi yivi* signifies insanity or mental illness, which is signified by not consistently maintaining the crown.

Crisply lined up, crisscrossed, and diamond-shaped parts in the hair indicate hair that is well controlled. Long and abundant hair is a sign of productive growing spirit, since all water people have spectacular hair. During initiation, Mande girls reside with spirits who teach them how to create stupefying, beautiful, and mysterious hairstyles considered inhuman because of their intricate designs.

Spiritual Protection and Containment

I prefer to have my head wrapped when doing any type of exorcism or spiritual banishing work. This is because I do not want bad spirits in my head or hair. Locs (dreadlocks), which is how I keep my hair, are believed to be energetic and behave as spiritual conduits, and it is important to protect them from collecting negative energy. Some people prefer their head covered with wide straw hats or head wraps when going into nature, for many practical or spiritual reasons.

Beautiful Cooling Medicine: Henna and Mehendi

One of the most spectacular, if temporary, methods of beautifying while enhancing spiritual wellness is through Mehendi. The art of Mehendi uses henna to create "temporary tattoos." Mehendi accentuates natural attractiveness and binds mind, body, and spiritual medicine into a singular experience. Mehendi is wildly popular in many parts of Africa and the diaspora, including South Africa, Kenya, the Sudan, Egypt, and the United States. You can find henna at your local Middle Eastern or Indian grocery store, through the henna supply directory online *www.hennapage.com*, or at your local health food store or herb shop.

Henna is said to:

> Bring good fortune, health, protection, and fertility.

> Be both inspirational and sensual, causing romantic and erotic dreams and becoming a powerful aphrodisiac when used in attraction magick.

> Be linked to the Great Mother, angels, and the element of fire.

> Transform the body into an alluring yet powerful natural talisman.

> Bring you, the wearer, into contact with deity and the elements, helping you identify and connect with the sacred in everyday life.

> Make you both look and *feel* beautiful by cultivating joie de vivre (joy of living).

Often in the United States, we like the shortcut and prefer the bare-bone facts; in our fast-paced world, such brevity helps us efficiently assimilate information. If we were to skim henna's surface in that manner, simply thinking it is one of two things (hair dye or temporary tattoo from a package), we would miss the real gift of this plant, which is its healing energy. Henna is a medicinal herb with many potent and promising qualities. It is, for example:

> An antipyretic (a natural coolant), hence its popularity in hot climates.

> An antispasmodic (soothing), antiseptic, astringent (drying), antibacterial, and antifungal.

> A natural sunscreen, which screens harmful chemicals, and effective for soothing sunburn when applied topically as a paste.

> A natural deodorant and antiperspirant, especially for the feet.

> A dye for the bottoms of the feet (a "step-in design") that insulates the foot from hot desert sands and serves as both a cheap and ornate substitute for sandals.

> An Ayurvedic medicine; henna tea is used as a beverage to treat many ailments including headache, fever, and stomach pain.

> A treatment for dermatitis (skin ailments), by cooling the skin.

> A curative for rheumatism, nervousness, and certain types of tumors, cancer, sexually transmitted diseases, and even leprosy in various folk traditions around the world.

> An aromatherapy scent, used to make *hina* perfume. *Gulhina* or *hina* perfume is purchased in small bottles (drams) of thick oil from health food stores and specialty Asian suppliers, and is a calming and balancing scent used by both men and women.

Henna and the Goddess

A henna artist is called a *negasseh* (*negasset*, plural). In a trance session, the negasseh uses connections with the spirit world to determine which patterns are needed. Various gods, goddesses, and spirits are encountered during the trance.

To be properly introduced to Mehendi and all of its magickal possibilities, it is important to visit a skilled negasseh, at least for the first time. Often they are not only gifted artists but are also adept intuitives who will create just the right pattern to enrich your life. Once you have experienced the magick of an accomplished negasseh, you will feel more confident about exploring henna on your own.

Ayurveda and Henna

Oils and waters added to henna do more than simply help its fluidity and staining ability. Ayurveda uses them in connection to the individual's particular dosha (body type). Ayurveda is an ancient method of healing from India that has also spread to cultures around the world, including many parts of Africa and the diaspora. In terms of the African diaspora, Ayurveda is particularly strong in influencing the healing ways of Jamaica, South Africa, and the United States.

Making and Using Henna

If you want to learn more about herbalism, the best way is hands-on, jumping in after making some preparations. See page 226 for a time-tested method I use for preparing henna for use as a Mehendi tattoo.

I consider eucalyptus and clove oil "must-haves" in a Mehendi recipe. Eucalyptus clears the head and purifies the air, and clove is grounding. The rose and orange blossom waters sweeten the affair, alleviating some of the medicinal scents of the essential oils.

You will need: paper towels, whisk, Pyrex bowl, sieve, four-quart pot, measuring cup and spoons, cotton ball, and a porcupine quill, bamboo skewer, dried lavender stalk, or plastic cone for application. Heat source: lit candle, burning loose incense such as frankincense and myrrh or kyphi, a cup of tea or soup. Also have on hand toilet paper, muslin, or gauze and a clean cotton sock.

Warning

While henna can be applied anywhere and even taken internally (if prepared by an Ayurvedic practitioner or herbalist), it is best known and most widely used as an application to the hair, hands, and feet.

Be Cautious about Unnatural Dyes

Deep, dark, natural henna enhanced with herbs and natural mordants is preferred over black henna to which dyes have been added. The origin of the latter is unknown and may damage the skin or cause serious allergic reactions.

When to Henna?

Henna is used from the beginning of life until its end at:
- Christenings
- Attraction rites
- Prenuptial rituals
- Weddings (by both bride and groom)
- Births
- Funerary rites

How to Do Mehendi

Cleanse areas to be treated very well with soapy water before beginning; dry thoroughly. Dip fingers, soles of the feet, or create an intuitive abstract pattern (the simpler the better). When the henna begins to dry, apply lemon-sugar blend with a cotton ball. Reapply lemon sugar every twenty minutes until a protective glaze forms. You can also use a porcupine quill for creating the designs (easily purchased from a beading supply shop or craft store), dried lavender stalk, or bamboo skewer to draw more intricate designs. Alternatively, you can spoon the henna mixture into a plastic cone or pastry cone. Most henna artisans prefer pastry-decorating tubes with very narrow tips to spread henna.

When glaze forms on the hennaed design, gently wrap hands or feet (wherever you've done the Mehendi) in gauze or toilet paper to protect designs. Be sure to keep hands or feet warm. Henna responds best to heat. This deepens its color and helps it stain longer. At this stage, I usually wrap my hands (or feet) in toilet paper, mummy-style, and then put them in a large pair of clean, old cotton socks. Alternatively, you can hold hennaed hands (or feet) near a lit fireplace, over a candle flame (far enough away so that you do not burn yourself or the wrapping, of course), or—the best yet—drink hot herbal tea you have on hand for this experience, such as rooibos, rose hip, or Assam or Ceylon with milk and honey or just lemon (holding the warm mug helps the henna to set).

Keep henna on your hands or feet as long as possible—four hours at the minimum, but overnight is preferred. Your dreams will be very interesting—I promise you that!

In the morning, flake off henna manually; do not use water in this process.

Massage hennaed areas with sesame oil but try to refrain from washing with soap for six hours. Pat with rose or orange blossom water if desired and towel blot.

HENNA RECIPE FOR MEHENDI

4 cups water

2 each: rose hip, rooibos, and Indian black tea bags (Assam or Ceylon)

2 tamarind pods

8-inch soft cinnamon stick

1 tablespoon apple cider vinegar

1 1/2 cups green henna powder[4]

1 tablespoon honey

1 teaspoon or so sesame oil (as desired)

1/2 cup rosewater

5 drops each eucalyptus and clove essential oils

1 ripe, juicy lemon

3 tablespoons white sugar

1 tablespoon orange blossom water

Bring water to a boil. Add tea bags to the pot. Open and scrape off the paste of the tamarind pods; add to pot along with the cinnamon stick broken into smaller pieces. Cover. Steep overnight. Add apple cider vinegar as mordant.

Pour approximately a cup of the green henna powder into a nonreactive (stainless steel or Pyrex) bowl. Sift three times to remove debris and refine. Microwave herbal tea mix for three minutes; whisk to mix well; strain through a sieve covered with a paper towel, and then add to the henna powder. Stir to form a thick paste. (Add liquid slowly so that mix doesn't become watery.)

Stir in honey, sesame oil, and rosewater, then essential oils. Eucalyptus helps skin receive the color and clove aids penetration ability of the henna. Let sit for two hours so color can mature (but keep at room temperature; do not refrigerate). Add more warmed liquid (tea mix or floral hydrosol—also called rose water, orange flower water, and lavender water) or more henna until you have achieved the desired smooth but pasty Greek-style-yogurt consistency; that is, the consistency of icing with the fluidity of the yogurt.

Lemon Sugar Glaze (for temporary tattoo)
While maturing henna batch, create a lemon sugar glaze. Squeeze and strain the juice of the lemon (remove seeds and discard). Add white sugar and stir. Add orange blossom water, so the mixture is thin but not excessively watery. Set aside.

How to Apply Hair Dye

WARNING: Must be used on uncolored, untreated hair and clean dry hair no more than one-quarter gray.

Start by parting hair into small sections. Completely saturate the hair shaft from root to ends with the henna paste—rub it in gently, then twist or clip and move this completely covered hair atop the head before carrying on with the next section of hair. Repeat until finished. Put on shower cap or tin foil to keep in heat. Sit out in the sun if possible or under a dryer placed on lowest heat setting for 40 minutes. Leave henna on as long as possible (at least one hour). Rinse thoroughly; condition very well because henna can be very drying (do not shampoo to rinse). Style as usual.

Henna Hair Tips

Henna is not recommended for hair more than one-quarter gray. It may be too strong and overwhelm very light, true-blond hair, so it may be best to avoid. Some packaged hennas are designed to lend strawberry blond colors, however.

To use packaged henna, follow manufacturer's directions and enhance as follows:

> Shampoo hair first.
> Bring out red tones by using cognac, red wine, carrot juice, cranberry juice, hibiscus tea, or rosehip tea in place of water.
> Tint and scent: add vanilla extract for scent or any combination of ground allspice, cinnamon, or cloves for enriched brown tones. Limit spices to a teaspoon. Avoid use on abraded scalp or on sensitive or allergic individuals.
> Minimize brassiness; use strong black coffee or rosemary, sage, or black tea in place of the water; especially good for brunette and black-haired beauties.
> For body, add flat beer or hops tea in place of water.
> Quench dryness with the addition of mayonnaise.
> Attract moisture with yogurt, sour cream, honey, or molasses.
> Follow up with a hot oil treatment to counteract dryness.

Henna for the Head

The most notable qualities of henna for hair and scalp:

> Amps up volume and builds body

> Decreases chemical and greasy buildups

> Emphasizes shine

> Develops subtlety in hue and tone

> Yields creative colors (avoids "out of the box" tired look)

> Excellent conditioner for all hair types

> Good for sensitive and irritated scalp, and can be an effective wound healer

> Reliable natural colorant for kinky, curly, wavy, and thick hair, which may be resistant to other types of dyes

> Inexpensive and widely available, henna is also a sustainable, natural, renewable-sourced herb.

Henna Medicine for the Mind, Body, and Spirit

One of the most revered qualities of henna is its ability to cool—that is why I call it cool medicine. It is a good idea to reflect on the cooling qualities of henna herb:

> Henna is a cooling plant that aids with numerous medical disorders.

> The soothing patterns of Mehendi tattoos are considered to be a calming influence that uplifts depression.

> Applying henna to the head cools down hotheaded thoughts, slows you down, and helps restore balance while instilling relaxation and tranquility.

> Doing Mehendi or applying henna hair dye instills patience and quells anxiety while alleviating stress.

> Mehendi and dyeing hair with henna invite communal activity, as either is difficult to accomplish alone—best shared with family or friends.

Take my lead, as my Mehendi-fingers glide back and forth across the keyboard (wish you could see them), bringing this chapter to a close for you. Allow henna to imbue your life with its holistic health benefits, uplifting mind, body, and spirit with happiness, filling your heart and home with joy. Life is short. Henna forces us to slow down. Take some time with family or friends while enjoying its healing medicine.

Temporary Tattoos
(books, kits, stencils, henna herb, and more)

mehandi.com

The Henna Page: *hennapage.com*

The sources sought for tribal beauty and championed in this chapter come naturally from Mother Earth. These sources are not beautifiers alone but enhance what we inherited from the ancestors and nature spirit. Tribal beauty embraces sustainable and renewable enhancement sources to accentuate the best of what we have. Many of the helpful phytomedicines featured in this chapter are from the Motherland, Americas, and Caribbean. By supporting the small women-operated entrepreneurial enterprises that make products from these phytomedicines, we help maintain biodiversity, strengthen fragile rural economies, and enrich our planet.

Henna Products Highlights

Aubrey Organics Egyptian Henna Shine-enhancing
Shampoo

Klorane Henna Shampoo from France

Nature's Gate Rainwater Henna Shampoo and
Conditioner

Hennalucent (variety of henna-based hair colors)

Gulhina Perfume (Attar from Henna) Tigerflag Natural
Perfumery: Pure Gulhina Attar, which is a symbiotic
blend of henna flower perfume and sandalwood
oil and is found on various websites from EBay to
Amazon.

CONCLUSION

Healing Power of African American Spirituality is an epochal exploration into the meaning of soul in sacred and mundane life of Africans in the diaspora with spiritual lessons for all. This book is also an investigation into the nexus of heart, art, and soul—how the three can come together to imbue life with unfathomably rich possibilities. The trio's possibilities include depth of loving, potential for healing the self and others, as well as the idea of tapping into energy that enriches the soul experience. As the journey of this book comes to an end, your possibilities for expanding, interacting with, and getting to know your soul are only beginning. Please take a few breaths and start your own pages of writing or sketching reflections of ideas for enriching your soul.

Ashe!

ENDNOTES

Chapter 1

1. Margarite Fernañdez Olmos and Lizabeth Paravisini-Gebert, *Creole Religions of the Caribbean* (New York: New York University Press, 2003), 22.

Chapter 3

1. These accounts of the role of midwives in the community as holistic health advisors as well as birth assistants come from numerous sources. Some of the more widely read include: Loudell F. Snow, *Walkin' Over Medicine* (San Francisco, CA: Westview Press, 1993); Debra A. Susie, *In the Way of Our Grandmothers: A Cultural View of Twentieth-Century Midwifery in Florida* (Athens, GA: University of Georgia Press, 1988); Katherine Clark and Onnie Lee Logan, *Motherwit: An Alabama Midwife's Story* (New York: EP Dutton, 1988).

2. "They" refers to black women, though this most likely included mixed race and Native American women as well.

3. Katherine Clark and Onnie Lee Logan, *Motherwit: An Alabama Midwife's Story* (New York: EP Dutton, 1988), 57.

4. Clark, *Motherwit*, 56.

5. Ibid., 58.

6. Reference to African American fear of doctors and their biomedicines.

7. See chapter 4, "Red: The Strength and Power of Blood," part 6, p. 64.

8. Loudell Snow, *Walkin' Over Medicine* (Boulder/San Francisco/ Oxford: Westview Press, 1933), 267.

9. Janette Y. Taylor, "Talking back: Research as an act of resistance and healing for African American women survivors of intimate male partner violence," *Women & Therapy* 25(34); published simultaneously in the anthology *Violence in the Lives of Black Women: Battered, Black and Blue*, ed. Carolyn M. West (New York: Haworth Press, 2002), 145–160.

Chapter 4

1. Barbara Walker, *The Woman's Encyclopedia of Myths and Secrets* (Edison, NJ: Castle Books, 1991), 375.

2. Ibid., 376.

3. Aruilla Payne-Jackson, Mervyn C. Alleyne, *Jamaican Folk Medicine* (University of West Indies Press, 2004), 89.

4. Ibid.

5. James A. Joseph, Daniel Nadeau, and Anne Underwood, *Color Code: A Revolutionary Eating Plan for Optimum Health* (New York: Hyperion, 2002), 30.

6. Ibid.,

7. Ibid.

8. Jean Carper, *Food—Your Miracle Medicine* (New York: HarperCollins, 1993), 449.

9. Anthony D. Buckley, *Yoruba Medicine* (Brooklyn, NY: Athelia Henrietta Press, 1997), 55.

10. Daniel K. Abbiw, *Useful Plants of Ghana: West African Uses of Wild and Cultivated Plants* (London: Intermediate Technology Publications, 1995), 190.

11. Ibid., 173.

12. Eve Palmer, *The South African Herbal* (Cape Town, South Africa: Tafelberg, 1985).

13. D. J. Cobb, "Red Bush Blessings," in *Llewellyn's Herbal Almanac* (St. Paul, MN: Llewellyn, 2005), 266–267.

14. Ibid., 267.

15. Loufy Boulos, *Medical Plants of North America* (Algonac, MI: Reference Publications, 1983), 155.

16. Buckley, *Yoruba Medicine*, 225.

17. Tami Hultman (ed), *The Africa News Cookbook: African Cooking for Western Kitchens* (New York: Penguin, 1985).

18. Palmer, *The South African Herbal*, 157.

19. Boulos, *Medical Plants of North America*, 25.

20. African American healers are called treaters in certain parishes of southwestern Louisiana.

21. Wonda L. Fontenot, *Secret Doctors: Ethnomedicine of African Americans* (Westport, CT: Bergin & Garvey, 1992), 18–121.

22. Carper, *Food*, 480.

23. This refers to physical health not the spiritual or mental benefits that have been traditionally associated with hawthorn berry as a charm and natural amulet for a variety of magickal purposes.

24. Expanded Commission E report of *The Complete German Commission E Monographs: Therapeutic Guide to Herbal Medicines*,

ed. Mark Blumenthal (Austin, TX: American Botanical Council; Boston: Integrative Medicine Communications, 1998).

25. Victoria Zak, *20,000 Secrets of Tea* (New York: Dell, 1999).

Chapter 5

1. From the Odu of Ifa, the word of Osayin as told by the griot.

2. Ibid.

3. William Ed Grime, *Ethno-Botany of the Black Americans* (Algonac, MI: Reference Publications, 1979), 12–13.

4. Ibid., 137–138.

5. Toby and Will Musgrave, *An Empire of Plants: People and Plants that Changed the World* (London: Cassel, 2000).

6. James K. McNair, *James McNair's Squash Cookbook* (San Francisco, CA: Chronicle Books, 1989), 54.

7. R. L. Zhou and J. C. Zhang, "An analysis of combined desensitizing acupoints therapy in 419 cases of allergic rhinitis accompanying asthma," *Chung Kuo Chung His I Chieh Ho Tsa Chih* 17(10):587–589.

8. M. Weiser, L. H. Gegenheimer, and P. A. Klein, "A randomized equivalence trial comparing the efficacy and safety of Luffa comp.-Heel nasal spray with cromolyn sodium spray in the treatment of seasonal allergic rhinitis," *Forsch Komplementarmed* 6(1999):142–148.

9. Daniel K. Abbiw, *Useful Plants of Ghana: West African Uses of Wild and Cultivated Plants* (London: Intermediate Technology Publications, 1995), 110.

10. Ibid.

11. Grime, *Ethno-Botany of the Black Americans,* 53.

12. Jean Carper, *Food—Your Miracle Medicine* (New York: HarperCollins, 1993).

13. Expanded Commission E report of *The Complete German Commission E Monographs: Therapeutic Guide to Herbal Medicines*, ed. Mark Blumenthal (Austin, TX: American Botanical Council; Boston: Integrative Medicine Communications, 1998).

14. Richard Katz, *Boiling Energy: Community Healing among the Kalahari Kung* (Cambridge, MA: Harvard University Press, 1982).

15. Jonathan D. Sauer, *Historical Geography of Crop Plants: A Select Roster* (Boca Raton, FL: CRC Press, 1993); Ben-Erik Van Wyk and Nigel Gericke, *People's Plants: A Guide to Useful Plants of Southern Africa* (Pretoria, South Africa: Briza Publications, 2000).

16. Ibid., 487.

17. Ibid.

18. Ibid., 482.

19. Ibid.

20. Callaloo Greens have to be cooked in a special way because of their high calcium oxalate content.

21. James A. Joseph, Daniel Nadeau, and Anne Underwood, *Color Code: A Revolutionary Eating Plan for Optimum Health* (New York: Hyperion, 2002), 112.

22. Lorenzo Dow Turner, *Africanisms in the Gullah Dialect* (New York: Arno Press, 1969).

23. Grime, *Ethno-botany of the Black Americans*, 19.

24. Joseph, *Color Code*, 117.

25. Abbiw, *Useful Plants of Ghana*, 38.

26. Faith Mitchell, *Hoodoo Medicine: Gullah Herbal Remedies* (Columbia, SC: Summerhouse Press, 1999), 84.

27. Carper, *Food*, 258.

28. Sue Monk Kidd, *The Secret Life of Bees* (New York: Penguin, 2003), 268–271.

29. Colin M. Turnbull, *The Forest People: A Study of the Pygmies of the Congo* (New York: Simon & Schuster, 1962), 276–277.

30. Yaya Diallo and Mitchell Hall, *The Healing Drum: African Wisdom Teachings* (Rochester, VT: Destiny Books, 1989), 30.

31. It is important to take note, honey is a serious allergen for some individuals; honey is contraindicated for nursing mothers and babies who are not yet immune to some of the bacteria it contains.

32. S. Fujiwara, et al., "A potent antibacterial protein in royal jelly: Purification and determination of the primary structure of royalisin," *Journal of Biological Chemistry* 265(1990):11,333–11,337.

33. T. Tamura, A. Fujii, and N. Kuboyama, "Antitumor effects of royal jelly (RJ)." *Nippon Yakurigaku Zasshji. Folia Pharmacologica Japonica* 89(1987):73–80.

Chapter 6

1. Moses Akin Makinde, *African Philosophy, Culture, and Traditional Medicine* (Athens, OH: Ohio University Center for International Studies, 1988), 110.

2. *Phyto* means "plant" and sterols are steroid constituents.

3. A sustainability organization.

4. Wildcrafting means harvesting a plant from the wild.

5. Beta-carotene is also referred to as vegetable vitamin A. Sweet potatoes are high in potassium as well. Collard greens are rich in both potassium and beta-carotene.

6. Research study by Ronald R. Watson, PhD, University of Arizona.

Chapter 7

1. Research study by Ronald R. Watson, PhD, University of Arizona, 8.
2. Ibid., 20.
3. Ibid., 21.
4. Edmund Asare, "Traditional knowledge in forest conservation: Case study of the Malshegu community in Ghana," Tampere Polytechnic, Finland, 2002.
5. T. Packenham, *Remarkable Trees of the World* (New York: W.W. Norton, 2003), 142.

Chapter 9

1. Barbara Walker, *The Woman's Encyclopedia of Myths and Secrets* (Edison, NJ: Castle Books, 1991), 886.
2. J. Arndt, "Salt from the Promised Land helps psoriasis patients," *Arzthliche Praxis* 34, 48; I. Machtey, "Dead Sea balneotherapy in osteoarthritis," Professional International Seminar on Treatment of Rheumatic Diseases, 1982; source: Amy K. McNulty, PhD, Salt Information FAQ Sheet.
3. Kombu has been shown in some tests to interfere with thyroid function and contribute to the formation of goiters. It is not recommended for treatment of HIV/AIDS.
4. Numerous herbs are associated with each deity. This is an abbreviated listing highlighting fragrant herbs used magically and spiritually.
5. Ra Un Nefer Amen, *Metu Neter Vol. 1: The Great Oracle of Tehuti and the Egyptian System of Spiral Cultivation* (Brooklyn: Kamit Publications, 1990), 285.
6. Bala Ifa Karade, *The Handbook of Yoruba Religious Concepts* (San Francisco: Weiser Books, 1994), 37.

7. Amen, *Metu Neter*, 287.

8. Karade, *The Handbook of Yoruba Religious Concepts*, 32.

9. Amen, *Metu Neter*, 290.

10. Karade, *The Handbook of Yoruba Religious Concepts*, 24–37.

11. Ibid.

12. Amen, *Metu Neter*, 293.

13. Karade, *The Handbook of Yoruba Religious Concepts*, 24–37.

14. Amen, *Metu Neter*, 280.

Chapter 10

1. Red tone can be evident in all healthy African descended complexions, from the fairest to darkest hue, and is not limited to one or the other.

2. Anthony D. Buckley, *Yoruba Medicine* (Brooklyn, NY: Athelia Henrietta Press, 1997), 209.

3. Faith Mitchell, *Hoodoo Medicine: Gullah Herbal Remedies* (Columbia, SC: Summerhouse Press, 1999), 54.

4. Powdered henna leaves can be easily purchased in pure form from reliable herbal shops, health food stores, or herbal suppliers.

GLOSSARY

ab—the heart, in Egyptian medicine, considered "the heart-soul"; also means offering.

African derived religions (ADRs)—the types of spiritual practices found in the African diaspora, including Santeria, Obeah, Lucumi, Regla de Ocha, Orisa, and Quimbois.

African diaspora—places where people of African descent live; for example, in North America, the Caribbean, South America, and parts of Europe.

Africanism—African-derived or inspired cultural presence in traditions, language, and beliefs of a related culture, such as the African descended people of the Americas and Caribbean.

African traditional religions (ATRs)—the original (pre-Christian, pre-Islamic) religions of the indigenous sub-Saharan African people that include the Ile Ifa of the Yoruba people.

akashic—energy encouraging you to go outside your physical and spiritual body.

animism—attributing nature with being alive with spirit.

àṣẹ—West African word roughly meaning "spiritual blessing."

ashe—West African word that describes magickal forces and energies of the universe.

babalawo—healer, a "keeper of secrets" from Yoruban language and Ile Ifa practices.

balneotherapy—a manner of encouraging wellness and curing diseases, injuries, and other physical ailments through bathing or baths utilizing natural springs, mineral waters, or the ocean.

calabash—plant that produces gourds; highly symbolic plant in African tradition.

CAM—acronym that stands for complementary and alternative medicine, which covers a broad spectrum of healing ways not considered conventional Western medicine.

candle dressings—the use of oils and botanicals to increase the magickal potential of a candle.

Commission E—a group that studies herbs intensely and verifies their efficacy with evidence-based studies.

conjure—to summon using supernatural power, to influence or effect by metaphysical means.

daliluw—the series of recipes and techniques for mixing the various medicinal constituents for healing.

decoct—to extract medicines from roots, barks, or berries by simmering in water.

deva—in Hinduism and Buddhism, a goddess, god, "shining one," or divinity. According to Zoroastrianism, deva is one of an order of evil spirits. In New Age belief, a deva is often connected to a particular plant, natural object, or place and is not considered a negative or positive spirit but instead a source of knowledge.

encrustation—the result of feeding a power object; the object becomes encrusted with its power food.

etu—burnt medicine, a type of healing used in parts of West Africa (e.g., black soap).

feeding—includes paying attention and honoring a medicine bag by applying oils, minerals, powders, or herbs to enhance its power.

goddess trinity—the Triple Goddess is one of the two primary deities found in the neopagan religion of Wicca. She comprises three separate goddesses united: Maiden Goddess, the Mother Goddess, and the Crone Goddess, each of whom symbolizes a stage in the female life cycle.

Hoodoo—an eclectic group of multicultural practices heavily influenced by the Angola, Kongo, and Dahomey people of Africa. In the Americas, Hoodoo has been influenced somewhat by Native American spirituality, Qabalah, the Pennsylvania Dutch, early spiritualists, and European magick.

hydrotherapy—the therapeutic use of water in baths or natural bodies of water with submersion of a particular body part or entire body as in a whirlpool.

Jiridon—the West African science of trees practiced by hunters, shamans, and warriors. Masters of Jiridon are master herbalists and adept ecologists.

love draw—attracting loving partnerships.

Lwa—intermediary spirits of Vodou religion.

medicine bag—power objects imbued with ashe for addressing various ills, contained in a bag or pouch with bilongo (medicine) and a mooyo (soul).

mojo bag—a small bag of charms that serves as an amulet for a wide range of purposes.

nature spirits—spirits of nature such as trees, mountains, bodies of water, or stones.

neopaganism—any of various religious movements arising chiefly in the United Kingdom and the United States in the late twentieth century that combine worship of pagan nature deities, particularly of the earth, with witchcraft.

nyama—nature as a sacred whole.

Orishas—angelic beings often compared to gods or goddesses.

power object—an object such as a shield, mask, sculpture, amulet, or charm gifted by the power and energy of natural spirit.

pupa—Yoruban medicine term for herbs, vegetables, and fruits of specific symbolic relation to the blood.

sacred—1) set apart for worship or veneration; 2) space devoted entirely to a specific purpose; 3) regarding religious objects, rites, or spiritual practice.

shamanism—a wide array of traditional beliefs and practices found around the world with a major emphasis on communicating with the spirit world.

soul bag—see *medicine bag*.

spiritual prophylactics—protective charms, amulets, chants, affirmations, and prayers.

tincture—solution of herbs preserved in alcohol or glycerin.

Vodou—an awe-inspiring tradition of bringing together plant energy with divinity, spiritual, and personal energy; also spelled Vodun, Vodoun.

warrior herbs—herbs useful for the wounds, cuts, bleeding, and other ailments that a warrior might experience.

Wheel of the Year—pre-Christian schedule of the year that includes many astrological and agrarian observations, honored through ritual and ceremony.

wildcrafting—harvesting of herbs in the wild rather than from cultivated spaces.

ABOUT THE AUTHOR

Photo © Diana O. Rasche Photography

Stephanie Rose Bird, is the author of eight books. She holds a BFA cum laude from Temple University, Tyler School of Art and an MFA from the University of California at San Diego where she was a San Diego Opportunity Fellow. She was a professor of fine art at the School of the Art Institute of Chicago for many years. She has also taught at the Illinois Institute of Art, Chicago Botanic Gardens, and Garfield Conservatory. Bird works as an artist, herbalist, aromatherapist, and is sole proprietor of Almost Edible Natural Products. Her product line features herbal soap, incense, potpourri, bath salts, sachets and dream pillows.

As a Fulbright Senior Scholar, Bird studied the art, rituals, and ceremonies of Australian Aborigines in the outback of the Northern Territory as a field researcher. Bird's fine art is held in several important national and international art collections; she has exhibited in numerous galleries, museums, universities and public spaces. Visit her at *www.stephanierosebird.com*.

Hampton Roads Publishing Company

. . . for the evolving human spirit

Hampton Roads Publishing Company
publishes books on a variety of subjects,
including spirituality, health,
and other related topics.

For a copy of our latest trade catalog,
call (978) 465-0504 or visit our distributor's
website at *www.redwheelweiser.com.* You can also
sign up for our newsletter and special offers by
going to *www.redwheelweiser.com/newsletter/.*